DECORATIVE

MAPS

RODERICK BARRON

BRACKEN BOOKS
LONDON

ACKNOWLEDGEMENTS
THE AUTHOR WOULD LIKE TO EXPRESS HIS THANKS TO JONATHAN POTTER
FOR HIS HELP, SUPPORT AND CO-OPERATION; TO TONY CAMPBELL, PETER BARBER
AND THE STAFF OF THE MAP LIBRARY AND DEPARTMENT OF MANUSCRIPTS
AT THE BRITISH LIBRARY, AND LAST BUT NOT LEAST THANKS TO HIS WIFE KATHRYN
FOR HER ASSISTANCE AND SUPPORT THROUGHOUT.

PUBLISHED BY BRACKEN BOOKS
AN IMPRINT OF BESTSELLER PUBLICATIONS LTD.
PRINCESS HOUSE, 50 EASTCASTLE STREET
LONDON W1N 7AP
ENGLAND

DECORATIVE MAPS
REPRODUCES A SELECTION OF PLATES AND ORIGINALS FROM
THE BRITISH LIBRARY
GREAT RUSSELL STREET
LONDON WC1 3DG
AND
JONATHAN POTTER LTD.
21 GROSVENOR STREET
MAYFAIR
LONDON W1X 9FE

POSTER ART SERIES

DECORATIVE MAPS
IS A VOLUME IN THE POSTER ART SERIES.
UP TO TEN PLATES MAY BE REPRODUCED
IN ANY ONE PROJECT OR PUBLICATION,
WITHOUT SPECIAL PERMISSION AND FREE OF CHARGE.
WHEREVER POSSIBLE THE AUTHOR, TITLE AND PUBLISHER
SHOULD BE ACKNOWLEDGED IN A CREDIT NOTE.
FOR PERMISSION TO MAKE MORE EXTENSIVE USE OF
THE PLATES IN THIS BOOK APPLICATION MUST BE MADE
TO THE PUBLISHER.

ISBN 1 85170 298 9

PRINTED IN ITALY

INTRODUCTION

'The Hereford Mappa Mundi for Sale.'

So read the newspaper headlines in the winter of 1988. Until that time few, if any, of us would have heard of this, one of our greatest national cartographic treasures, let alone known exactly what it was.

In about the year 1300 Richard of Haldingham produced this spectacular vision of the medieval Christian world which is now preserved in the ancient cathedral at Hereford. Its rise from obscurity has, as it were, put cartography back on the map. As one of the earliest, rarest and finest examples of its type, it is the starting-point for our survey of a visual and artistic tradition which covers over five centuries and demonstrates man's enduring fascination with the art of producing maps. Mapmaking, as we will see, brings together a whole host of academic and artistic disciplines — the study of history and geography; art and design; calligraphy, heraldry and genealogy, draughtsmanship and colouring — all of which combined to produce one of the most decorative yet still underestimated of arts.

DESIGN AND FORM

The invention of printing in the middle years of the fifteenth century transformed the art of producing maps. Up to that time all known maps had been produced painstakingly by hand, and there had evolved two quite distinct traditions.

The Hereford 'mappa mundi' is one of the finest examples of the scholarly ecclesiastical tradition. In the early Middle Ages the Church remained the guardian of scholarship and knowledge. Rich monastic libraries throughout Europe provided the medieval cleric and scholar with access to information that was essentially Christian in outlook and limited in its geographical knowledge. The types of map that evolved in the early Middle Ages, like the Hereford world map, were not necessarily the latest and most up-to-date maps of the known world. In many cases Jerusalem was shown at the centre, representing the centre of Christendom, a symbol of the Church at the centre of peoples' daily lives. The content of the maps also provided a visual encyclopaedia of Christian and Biblical knowledge onto which was added the limited geographical knowledge of a very circumscribed European world.

By contrast, the practicalities of navigating Europe's inland sea — the Mediterranean — led to the emergence of a quite separate tradition, that of the portolano or sailing chart. Produced on the skins or hides of animals, these types of map began to appear in the early fourteenth century with the emergence of independent commercially orientated nation-states along the shores of the northern Mediterranean. Until the Age of Discoveries their depictions were principally of the Mediterranean and they continued to provide exceptionally accurate navigational aids beyond the age of printing and well into the sixteenth and seventeenth centuries. The principal powers of Spain and Portugal had only limited knowledge of new printing processes, and the official shroud of secrecy that surrounded their discoveries in the New World and Indies made them reluctant to disseminate new information through printed maps to political and commercial rivals in Europe. The portolano became the official cartographic document of Spain and Portugal. Dynasties and generations of families were employed to produce visual reflections of Europe's expanding overseas empires. Royal patronage ensured that in most cases these were expensive and lavish works of art. Of those charts which were actually used by the seamen and navigators of the day the portolano was often preferred to new printed charts because of its durable and hardwearing qualities at sea.

Printed maps first appear in 1477 and were gradually refined through improvements in printing processes. Early wood-blocks provided a rather stark naïve image of the world which was only transformed in the sixteenth century with the use of copper plates on which to engrave maps; the refined line and quality achieved by the Dutch engravers of the seventeenth century has rightly given rise to the term 'the Golden Age'. Mapmakers like Blaeu, Hondius and Visscher brought mapmaking to new heights of excellence. Only in the nineteenth century, with industrialization and scientific advances, was a rival to this refinement found in steel engraving. Harder and longer-lasting steel gave even more scope to the artistry of the engraver and some of its finest exponents, John Tallis and Thomas Moule, are seen as the latter-day Blaeus of mapmaking.

COLOUR AND PRINT

Colour is an integral part of any map. From a monotone picture or engraving, it brings to life the finesse and content of the map.

For the early medieval cartographer-cleric, the colouring of maps involved all the same techniques as the intricate art of book illumination; indeed many mappa mundi like the Hereford world map are found in psalters and prayer-books of the period.

Using a quill or brush mineral pigments were applied to the vellum, often lightened or thickened by adding white lead. These could be bound by using ox bile, starch, egg whites or gum arabic, the latter producing a rich polished sheen. When available more expensive minerals were used, such as ultramarine (lapiz lazuli) and gold, which could be applied in sheets of gold leaf or as a powder bound with gum. This illuminator's art was handed on to the portolano chart-maker and in the charts of Sanches, Homem and Rotz (Plates 3, 4, 14) we see these same techniques being used.

The invention of printing made the production of maps and their colouring two quite separate processes. The map was published in black and white and might be sold coloured or uncoloured. Notable amongst the colouring of the early wood-block maps is the Ulm edition of Ptolemy's *Geographia* published in 1482 (Plate 2). Freshness and clarity are shown by a richness of light and dark blue which contrasts with other primary colours to provide a stunning visual effect.

The golden age of Dutch cartography gave rise to an independent map-colouring industry. The father of modern cartography, Abraham Ortelius (Plate 8), was trained not as a surveyor or cartographer but as a map-colourist. In his early years he worked with his sister servicing the burgeoning map business in the Netherlands. Indeed the production of multi-volume atlases of which Ortelius' *Theatrum* and Blaeu's *Atlas Maior* are amongst the finest, led to the emergence of specialist map-colourists like Adrian Van Santen. Like the portolanos these coloured maps were often for the libraries of royalty or nobility and consequently involved beautifully rich hues of water-based wash colours, often heightened with gold.

In 1701 John Smith in his *Art of Painting in Oyl* dedicated a whole chapter to 'The Whole Art and Mystery of Colouring Maps in Water Colours'. He noted that: 'The only way to colour maps well is by a pattern done by some good workman, of which the Dutch are esteemed the best.' In the period up to the nineteenth century there was, if anything, a movement away from rich colour towards a more functional application of colour, the aim being to depict the administrative and political divisions of a country rather than to beautify and embellish with cartouches and decorative details. Certainly the maps of John Tallis and Thomas Moule (Plates

38, 39, 40) are usually found with the original outline colour to define the political and administrative divisions.

LETTERING

As a formal element in the overall design of maps, lettering can be equally significant and expressive. Harmoniously positioned and combined with engraved detail and decorative design, it can be both functional and ornamental, enhancing the decorative quality of a map.

Until the late fifteenth century the Roman hand was the lettering of officials and scholars. This style is seen clearly in the Hereford Mappa Mundi and in the earliest wood-block maps, as well as the portolano chart of Jean Rotz. Much of the effect of the 1482 Ulm world map is based upon these heavy Roman capitals. By contrast on Rotz's map the small Roman letters are clearly secondary to the vivid pictorial image presented.

For the new commercial age of sixteenth- and seventeenth-century cartography, however, the Roman hand had many deficiencies. To write or engrave separate vertical letters was slow and labour-intensive. For mapmakers, letter-writers and administrators the flowing italic hand provided the answer, since it was smoother, more flexible, fluent and elegant in its style. Names could be written or engraved neatly and elaborated with ornamental flourishes.

One of the foremost proponents and exponents of this new italic hand was the famous cartographer Gerard Mercator. The influence of Mercator's work is seen most clearly amongst the maps of his contemporaries. His colleague Frans Hogenberg engraved maps in Mercator's own 'Atlas', and numerous maps for Abraham Ortelius' *Theatrum Orbis Terrarum* (1570), as well as for his joint project with Georg Braun, the first atlas of town plans, the *Civitates Orbis Terrarum* (1572). The elegance of the italic hand can be seen in Ortelius' map of the Americas (Plate 8) as well as the bird's-eye views of Frankfurt and Palmanuova (Plates 6, 10). This new style is also evident in Christopher Saxton's splendid map of Dorset (1579) (Plate 7). Although engraved in England many of the maps were the work of Flemish refugees, including Remigius Hogenberg, brother of Frans. The flamboyant title lettering is balanced by restrained and fluent place names.

Throughout the golden age of seventeenth-century cartography the italic hand was used as a complement to and juxtaposition for the more formal capital lettering of the title-pieces of maps; for example in John Speed's decorative maps of France and America (Plates 15, 16).

HERALDRY AND COATS OF ARMS

Early portolano charts of the Mediterranean and later of other parts of the world are perhaps the first examples of heraldry on maps. The cities and states of Europe are shown as pennants or flags or coats of arms, whilst the creeping influence of Islam in the East is represented by the Turkish crescent (Plates 4, 14).

Amongst the earliest printed maps to use coats of arms were those of Christopher Saxton in his *Atlas of England and Wales* (1579). All thirty-five maps in the atlas bear the coats of arms of Thomas Seckford, patron of his atlas and Member of Parliament for Ipswich, and the royal coat of arms of Queen Elizabeth to whom the work was dedicated (Plate 7).

John Speed, historian and antiquary, brought the decoration of heraldic devices on English county maps into common usage. His spectacular county atlas, first published in 1611, incorporated maps of each of the English and Welsh counties with the armorial bearings of its nobility, gentry and institutions past and present. His maps of Oxford and Cambridge (Plate 11) are amongst the most decorative, with the coats of arms of the universities' colleges around the borders of the maps.

Private patronage and subscription were an essential part of the seventeenth- and eighteenth-century mapmakers' existence. Often these were the only way of raising finance. Subscriptions would be sought from the wealthy and aristocratic classes, in return for which their arms and devices would be incorporated into the cartographer's maps. Examples of this can be seen in Herman Moll's flamboyant title cartouche for his map of Africa (Plate 33) and Moses Pitt's more restrained dedication to Charles Fitzcharles (Plate 29).

The Victorian period saw little of this tendency to embellish with coats of arms. There is one exception, Thomas Moule, an expert on the history of heraldry and author of an exhaustive survey on the heraldry of fish. Moule's county maps, first published in the *English Counties Delineated* (1836), incorporate the coats of arms of counties, towns, nobility and ancient institutions. They are quite atypical of an age where scientific accuracy and reporting were the keynotes of cartography. His map of Oxfordshire (Plate 38) harks back to the golden age of seventeenth-century cartography.

CARTOUCHES

An integral part of most printed maps particularly of the late sixteenth and seventeenth centuries were the decorative details which surrounded the titles, scales and keys.

Looking at those of Abraham Ortelius' map of America (Plate 8) and Christopher Saxton's map of Dorset (Plate 7) we can see noticeable similarities. Both maps were the work of Flemish engravers and both have an abstract strapwork design that incorporates faces, plants, birds and hanging chains and loops. The influence of the strapwork design continued into the seventeenth century with Jodocus Hondius' map of Japan (Plate 13).

Later maps of the seventeenth century take on a more realistic detail in the embellishment of cartouches. Joan Blaeu's map of Central Africa (Plate 21) depicts Ethiopians under the shade of parasols, whilst Louis Renard's spectacular chart of Europe (Plate 36) incorporates a central cartouche where playful cherubs demonstrate the scientific and navigational instruments of the day – the astrolabe, cross-staff and plumb line. Hendrick Doncker's Chart of the East Indies (Plate 35) provides a vivid array of images in the title cartouche which portray the 'mysteries of the Orient'.

REALISM: PEOPLE AND PLACES

This move towards a more realistic view of the world was not confined to the decorative detail of the map, nor was it something that emerged in the seventeenth-century heyday of mapmaking. Examine the bottom panels of the Hereford Mappa Mundi (Plate 1) and you will see a medieval pilgrim on horseback that might have come straight out of Chaucer. Jean Rotz's superb manuscript chart of South East Asia (Plate 3), depicts almost to the letter the account of the Parmentier brothers' visit to the coasts of Sumatra in 1529.

Laurence Nowell's manuscript map of England and Ireland (Plate 5) takes a more humourous attitude to realism. The mapmaker is shown in the bottom left corner of the map, sitting exhausted after his labours, assaulted by a barking greyhound. In the opposite corner his patron, William Cecil, Lord Burghley, sits impatiently, hour glass at hand, waiting for completion of his survey.

The consistent use of figures to elaborate and decorate really came to the fore in the late sixteenth and early seventeenth centuries. Braun and Hogenberg's atlas of town plans, the *Civitats Orbis Terrarum*, which first appeared in Cologne in 1572 (Plate 6), incorporated costumed figures into the foreground of the maps. The editors had laid this down from the commencement of the work. The aim was not only to illustrate the typical inhabitants of the towns. At a time when the Turks were still a considerable threat in central and south-eastern Europe, it was felt that the addition of human figures might discourage the Infidel, whose religion forbade him to gaze upon images which included human forms.

The *Civitates* was published as a companion work to Ortelius' *Theatrum*, and it was this link which brought the related fields of topographic drawing and map-making closer together. Braun and Hogenberg, writing of the task of the topographical draughtsman, stated: 'He describes each section of the world individually with its cities, villages, islands, rivers, lakes, mountains and springs and so on, tells its history, making everything so clear that the reader seems to be seeing the actual town or place before his eyes.' This desire to conjure up the very essence of a place or country, to put a mirror or 'eye-glass' on the world as many early seventeenth-century cartographers described it, led to the emergence of perhaps the most decorative of seventeenth-century map forms — the so-called 'carte-à-figures'. If we look at the maps of John Speed (Plates 15, 16), William Blaeu (Plate 22), Jodocus Hondius (Plate 20) and Frederick de Wit (Plate 25), we see a distinctive style of cartography where the content of the map is almost secondary to providing as full a visual image of the country as possible. People and costumes, places, flora and fauna, history and geography are all merged to provide 'mirrors' of the world, within the confines of the mapmaker's art.

The incorporation of topographical details within maps was to continue through to the nineteenth century. We can see the decorative appeal of this combination of images in the works of Allard, Pitt and Moll.

Latterly it was John Tallis and Thomas Moule who revived most fully the idea of a 'carte-à-figures'. In the age of steam and empire the Victorian armchair traveller could conjure up at a glance images of far-flung countries and not so far-flung English counties. Armchair tourism was on the map.

ANIMALS

The use of animals in maps was commonplace from the earliest times (Plate 1). Man's deepest fears and superstitions concerning wide expanses of uncharted seas and vast tracts of 'terra incognita' were reflected in the monstrous animals that have appeared on maps ever since the Mappa Mundi. The maps of Ortelius and his Dutch successors are filled with vignettes of spouting whales and ferocious fishes.

The Portuguese portolanos of Homem and Sanches (Plates 4, 14) also provide a more realistic view of African and South American wildlife including one of the earliest depictions of a rhinoceros. Blaeu (Plate 21) and Allard (Plate 34) were admirable observers of nature, Allard's map of New England providing a veritable zoo of North American wildlife. This move towards a more fullsome and realistic image of the world was greeted with some scepticism by the poet Jonathan Swift, writing in 1733:

> So Geographers in Africs maps
> With Savage Pictures fill their gaps
> And O'er unhabitable Downs
> Place Elephants for Want of Towns.

In general this is an exaggeration by Swift. Animals reflected both man's fears and later man's increasing awareness of the world around him but never reached the point of obliterating the information conveyed on the maps he produced.

IMAGES AND SYMBOLISM

We have already noted the centring of the Hereford world map on Jerusalem, and the idea of the medieval map as a microcosm of the real world. Whilst in early medieval Europe Jerusalem's recapture was the goal of most European clerics, Rome still held powerful sway in terms of its power, glory and Papal authority. Henricus Hondius' map of Italy conjures up the familiar image of the she-wolf suckling Romulus and Remus, the founders of Rome. The glory of Rome is vividly captured in Claes Janz Visscher's spectacular world map of 1652 (Plate 23), with twelve Roman emperors, in a line from Julius Caesar to Domitian.

Whilst the Ulm edition of Claudius Ptolemy's world map (Plate 2) was the result of a rediscovery of classical geography, many Dutch cartographers were quick to use the images not of classical geography but of mythology. The elements — earth, fire, air and water — were frequently represented on Dutch world maps of the seventeenth century with appropriate scenes from classical mythology (Plate 27).

Similarly, the continents take on allegorical forms. Claes Janz Visscher's world map supplies these in each of the corners of his map. The usual four elements and four continents provided the symmetry and balance which was so important to the artistry of seventeenth-century mapmaking. Examine Frederick de Wit and Herman Moll's maps of Africa and you will see Africa — the native astride an alligator — in both title cartouches (Plates 25, 33).

Perhaps one of the most curious sets of images and symbols is Andreas Cellarius' spectacular star chart (Plate 24). Maps of the heavens were familiar depictions in atlases from the sixteenth century onwards. We can recognize familiar symbols in Frederick de Wit's chart (Plate 30), yet Cellarius adopts a truly Christian outlook on the cosmos for this chart. The stars take on a Biblical quality and we have the Old and New Testament laid before us — Noah's Ark, Moses and the Tablets, the Adoration of the Magi, the fisherman Peter on Lake Gallilee, and the twelve Apostles replacing the twelve signs of the Zodiac.

THE CURIOSITY

Looked at in a modern context, part of the appeal of old maps is the amusement we derive from their strange outlines and orientations. Jodocus Hondius' map of Japan (Plate 13) and John Speed's and Louis Hennepin's maps of the Americas (Plates 16, 32) show Korea and California as islands, reflecting the uncertainties of early navigators and explorers, yet many maps were designed purely for decorative amusement.

Pieter Van den Keere's 'Leo Belgicus' (Plate 12) was one of a long series of maps which depicted the Low Countries in the form of a lion. The use of human and animal forms to depict countries perhaps reached its heights in late eighteenth- and early nineteenth-century England. Bowles' and Carver's 'Geography Bewitched' series of the countries of the British Isles was amongst the most popular, England a cheery beer-swilling fellow astride a fish, Scotland a Punch-like fellow seated on a cushion (Plate 37). The instructive and informative elements of cartography are here superceded by the desire to decorate and amuse.

CONCLUSION

Dr. John Dee, the Elizabethan mathematician wrote: 'Some to beautifie their Halls . . . or Libraries with, some others for their own journeys directing into far lands or to understand other mens' travels . . . liketh loveth, getteth and useth maps, charts and geographical globes.' Dee's statement is still as current today. The maps that follow will illuminate, illustrate and inform in a way that few others works of art find possible.

RODERICK BARRON

FEBRUARY 1989

PLATE 1

Richard of Haldingham: The Hereford Mappa Mundi

Few maps can compare with this remarkable pictorial encyclopaedia of medieval knowledge, created by a little-known scholar and cleric, Richard of Haldingham, in England about the year 1300. Derived somewhat circuitously from the Agrippa Map of the Roman Empire commissioned by Caesar Augustus (shown here in the bottom corner), in the first century AD, it is drawn on a circular model with Jerusalem at its centre. Some four feet in diameter, it shows the medieval world of Europe, Africa and Asia, where legends and fables contrast with Biblical scenes from Paradise to the Crucifixion. An extraordinary medieval masterpiece, and one of Britain's finest national treasures. (Collection: Hereford Cathedral. By courtesy of Dean and Chapter of Hereford Cathedral)

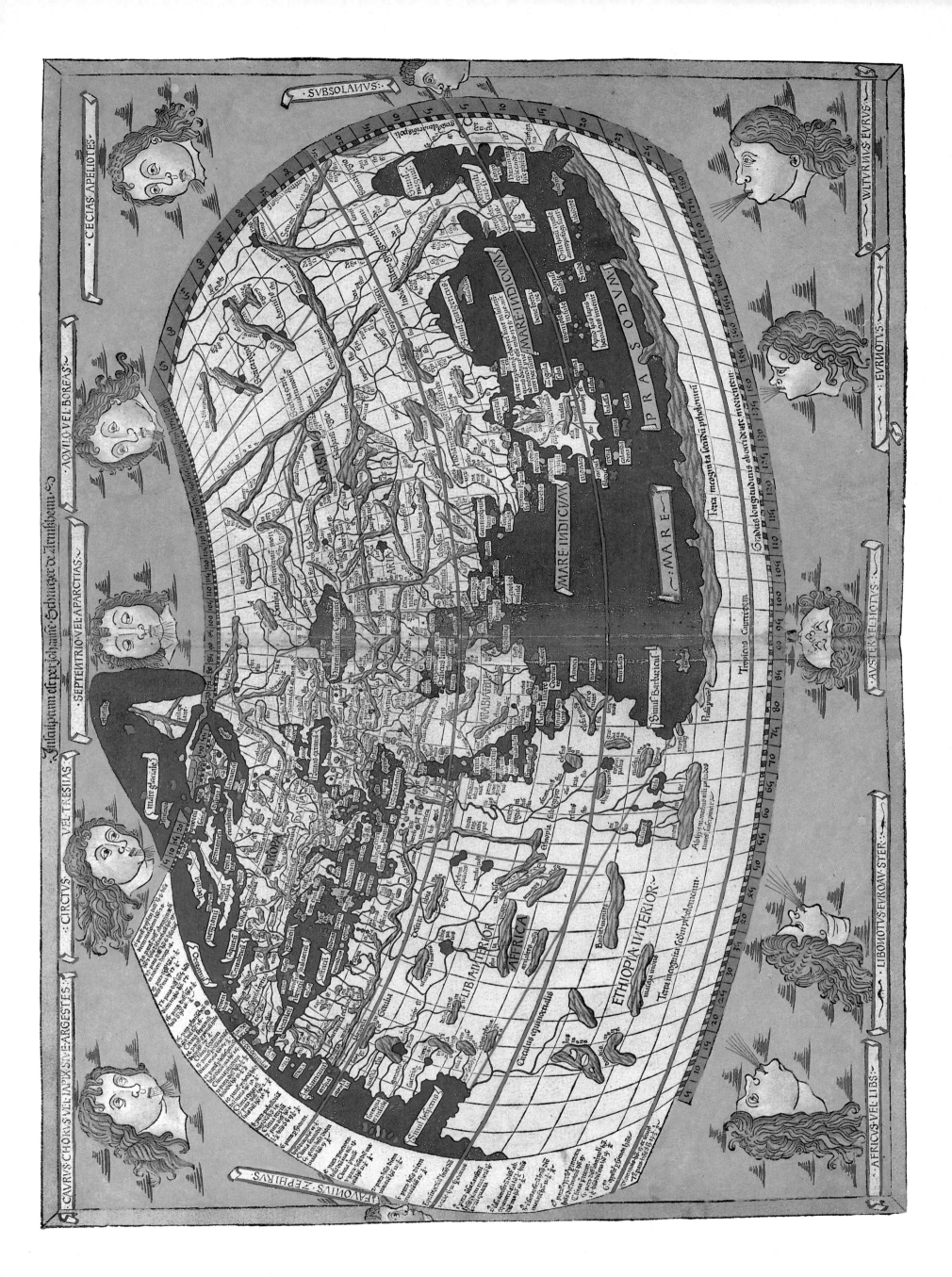

PLATE 2

Claudius Ptolemy: The World

Engraved by Johannes Schnitzer in Ulm in 1482, this stunning world map was based on the works of the second-century cartographer Claudius Ptolemy. It is a milestone in the history of mapmaking, being one of the first maps to be published north of the Alps and to show the medieval world on the dawn of the Age of Discoveries. (Collection: Jonathan Potter Ltd.)

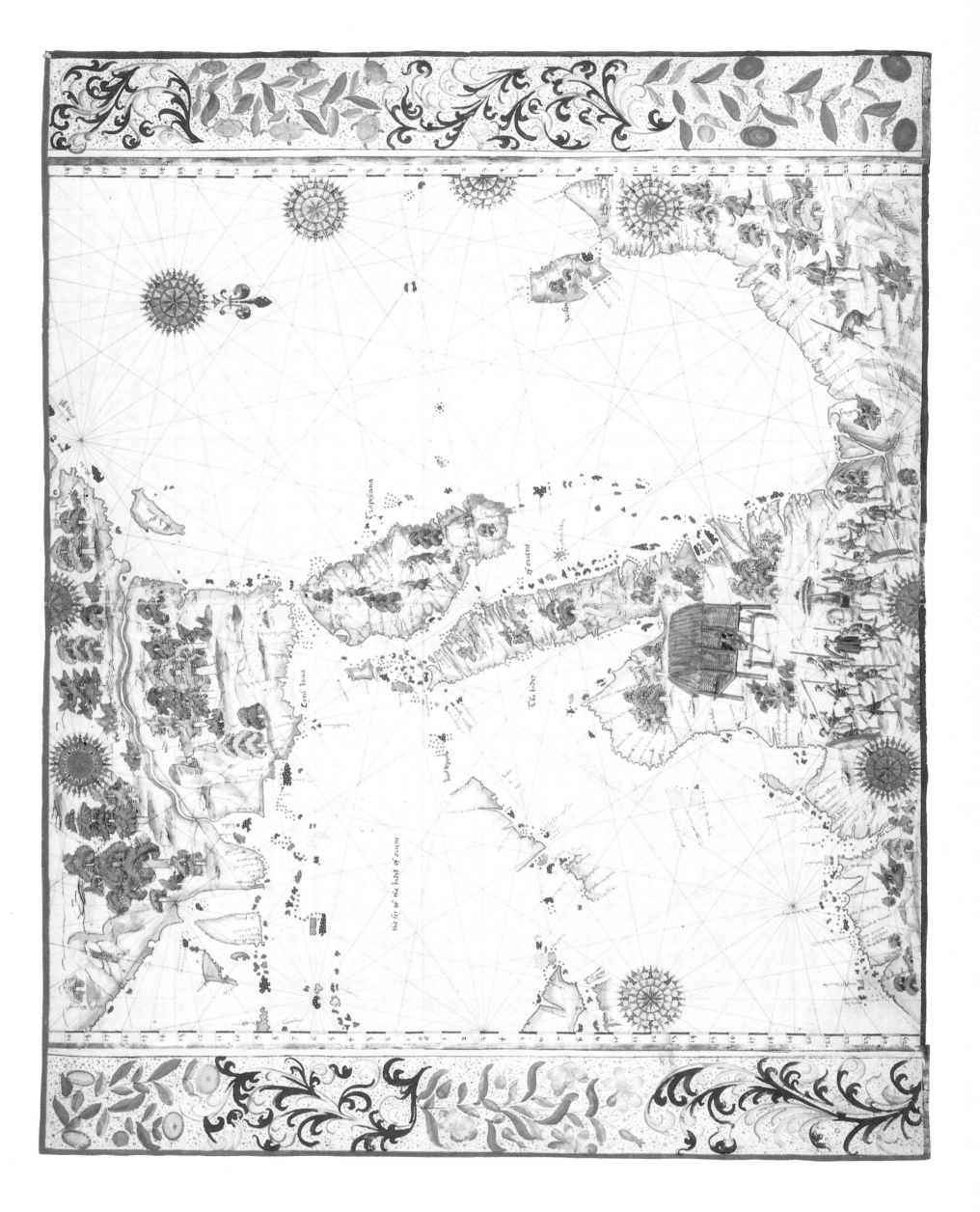

PLATE 4

Diego Homem: Portolan Chart of the Atlantic

Part of a lavish portolan atlas drawn by Diego Homem in 1558 and probably presented to Queen Mary of England, this chart of the Atlantic depicted an area of strategic importance to the Portuguese colonial and trading empires in Brazil and West Africa. The early development of the slave trade produced manpower and wealth as well as welcome ports of call for Portuguese vessels on their long arduous voyages to the Indies. (Collection: British Library)

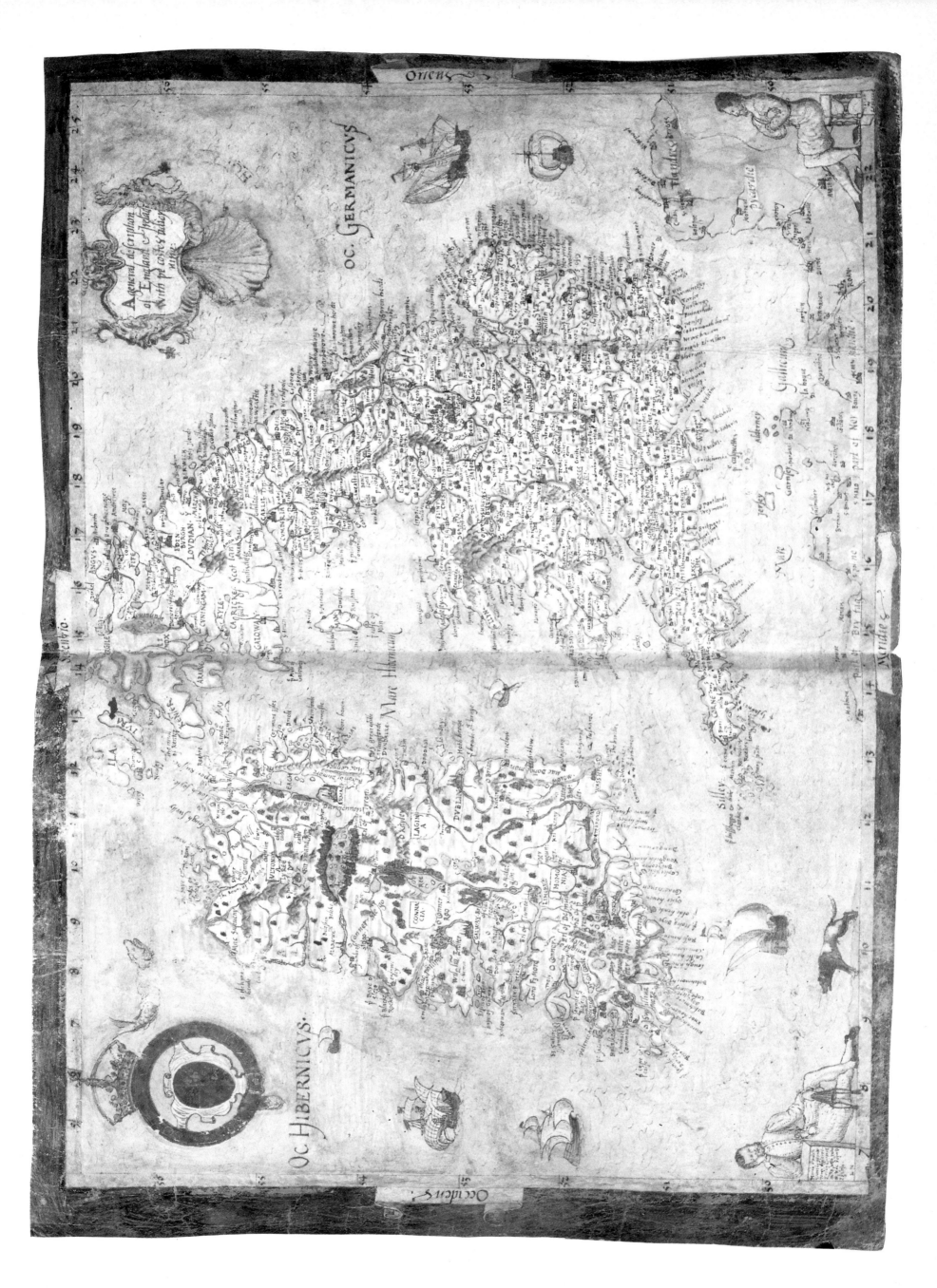

PLATE 5

Laurence Nowell: A General Description of England and Ireland

This exquisitely produced manuscript map by Laurence Nowell was, at the time of its creation in 1564, one of the most accurate depictions of the British Isles. The remarkable detail is embellished with charming portraits of the exhausted Nowell and his impatient patron and first owner of the map, William Cecil, Lord Burghley, Elizabeth I's Chief Minister. (Collection: British Library)

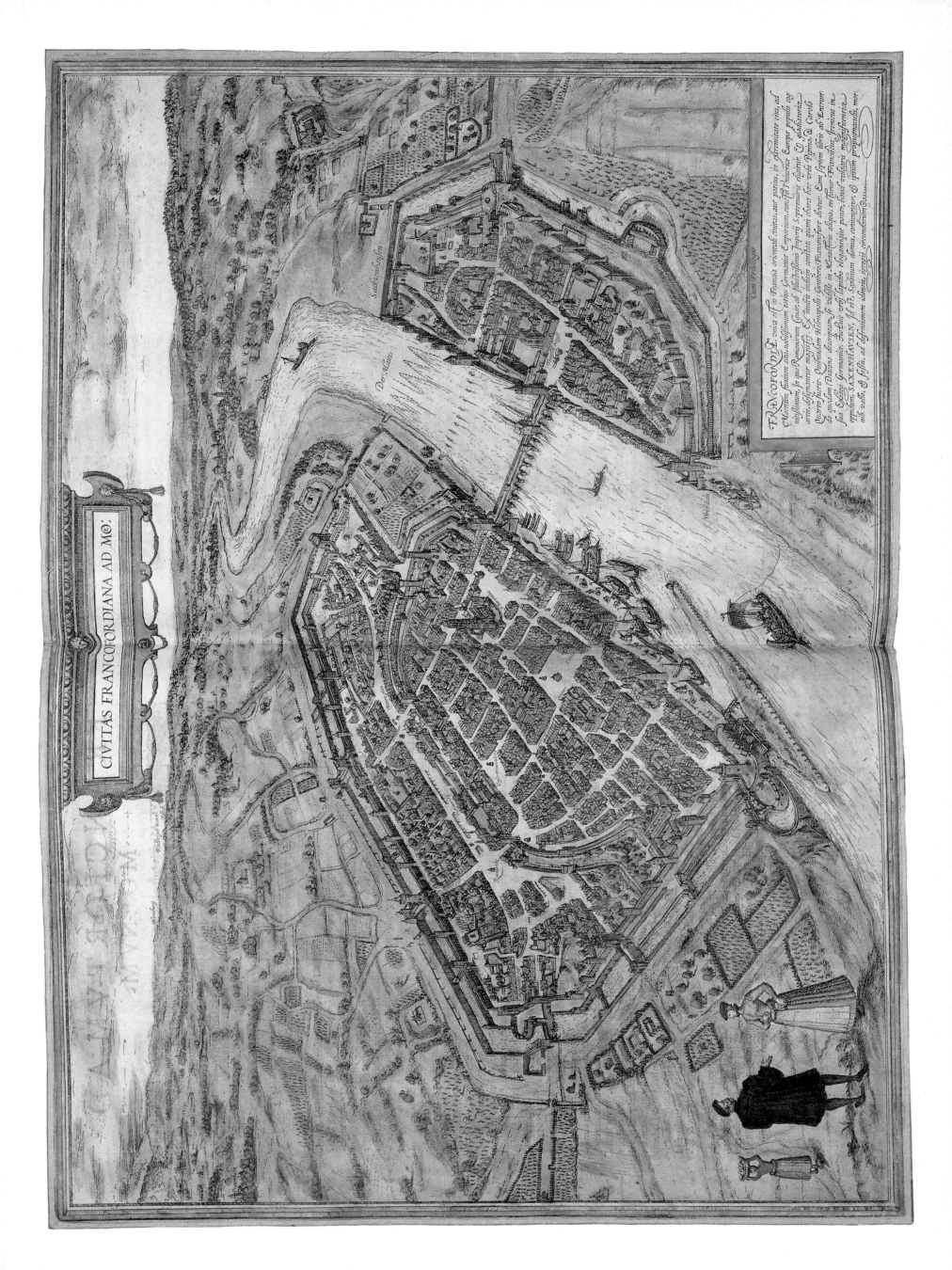

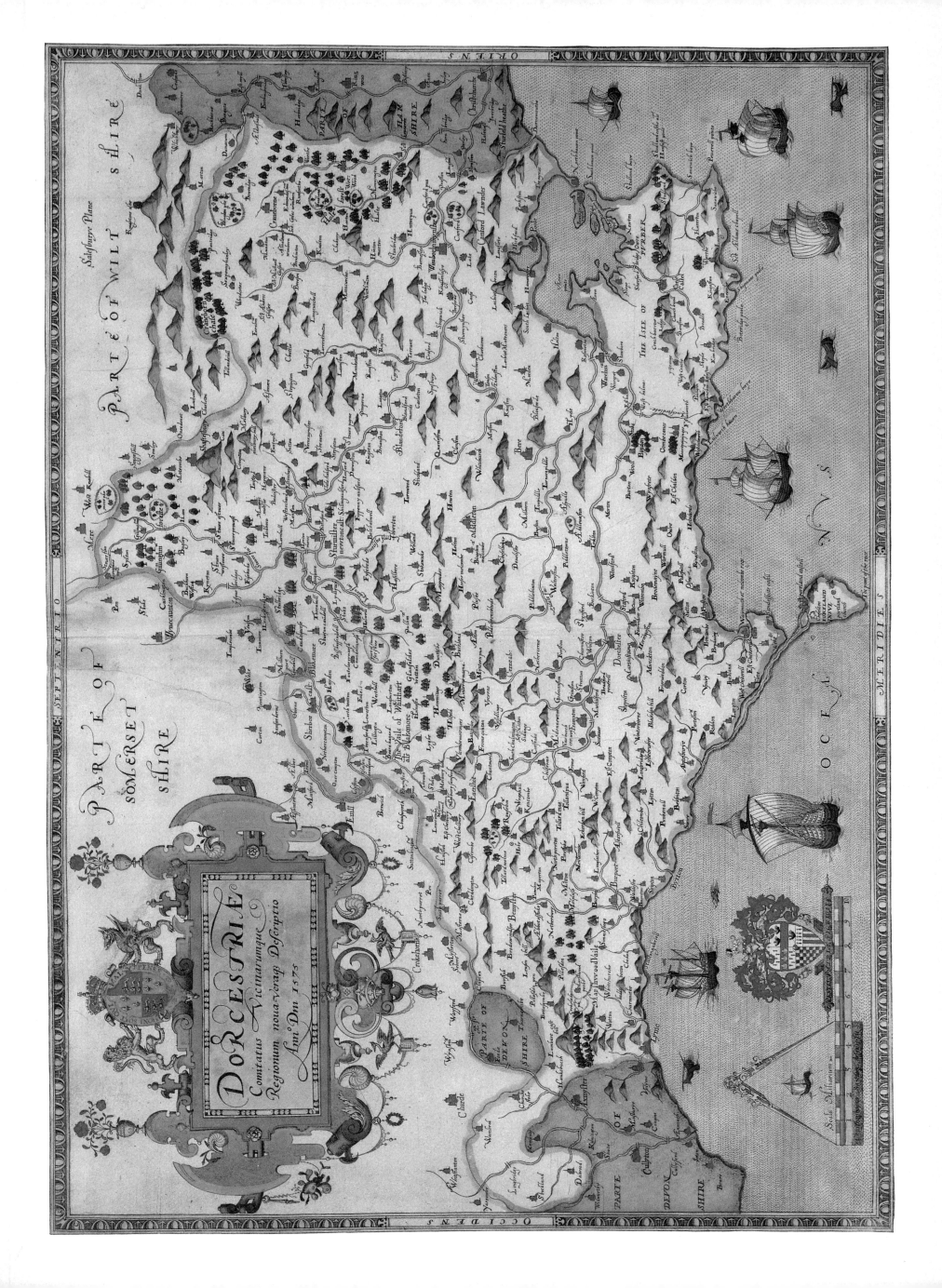

PLATE 7

Christopher Saxton: Dorcestriae

A milestone in the history of English mapmaking, Christopher Saxton's beautifully engraved map of Dorset is the first available printed map of this English county. It appeared in his Atlas of England and Wales, *the first systematic survey of Elizabeth I's realm published in 1579 in London. (Collection: Jonathan Potter Ltd.)*

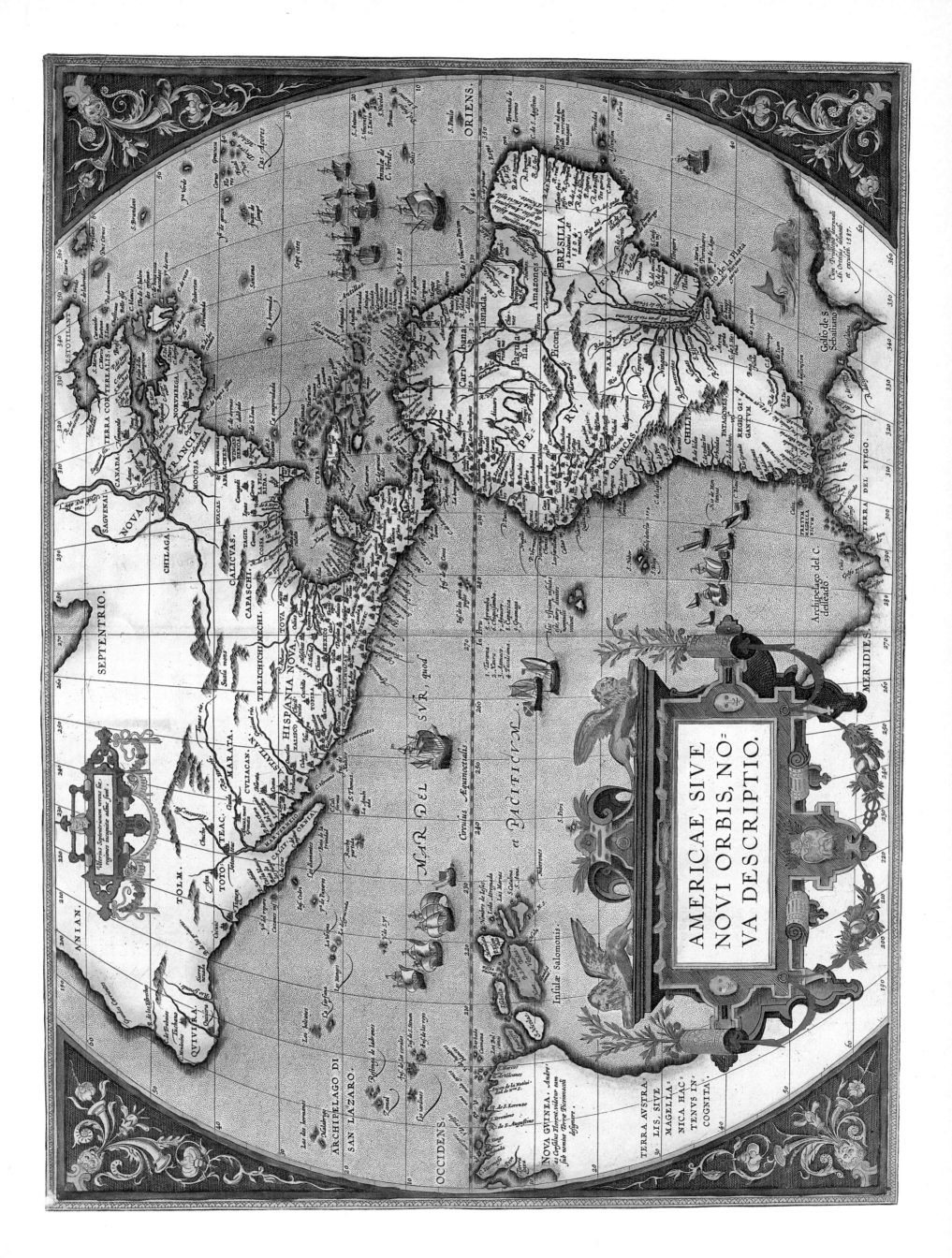

AMERICAE SIVE NOVI ORBIS, NOVA DESCRIPTIO.

PLATE 8

Abraham Ortelius: Americae Sive Novi Orbis Nova
Descriptio

*Abraham Ortelius is regarded by many as the father of modern
mapmaking. This beautifully engraved map of the Americas
appeared in his* Theatrum Orbis Terrarum, *the first
uniformly produced world atlas published in Antwerp in 1570.
Ortelius' wide range of sources provides us with one of the most
accurate images of the Americas only one hundred years after
Columbus. (Collection: Jonathan Potter Ltd.)*

THE true description or draught of that famous Ile of WIGHTE, with some parte of the Englishe or Britaine coast and inwards Countrye of HAMBSHIRE, and SVSSEX wherein Gentil Reader you maye See the true distances sett downe, by measure or Scale of anye parte therof, also the particuler descriptions of Hylls, Woodes, Beacons, Castells, Rockes, and Thinges, which vuto this plott are adioyninge. Made by Baptista Boazio. 1591.

Scale of Englifhe Myles.

BRITTANNE SEG

THE

PART OF SVSSEX

CHE CHESTER

PART OF HAMSHYRE

PART OF SOVTH HAMPTON

PLATE 10

Georg Braun and Frans Hogenberg: Palmanuova

A study in balance and symmetry this bird's eye view appeared in Cologne in 1598 in Georg Braun and Frans Hogenberg's famous atlas of town plans, the Civitates Orbis Terrarum, *and shows the City of Palmanuova in north-eastern Italy. Heavily fortified, it was built by the Venetians to protect the Adriatic coasts against the incursions of the Turks. (Collection: British Library)*

PLATE 11

John Speed: Cambridgeshire

Few English county maps can surpass this beautifully decorative map of the university county of Cambridgeshire, first published in London in John Speed's famous English County Atlas, The Theatre of the Empire of Great Britaine, *1611. (Collection: British Library)*

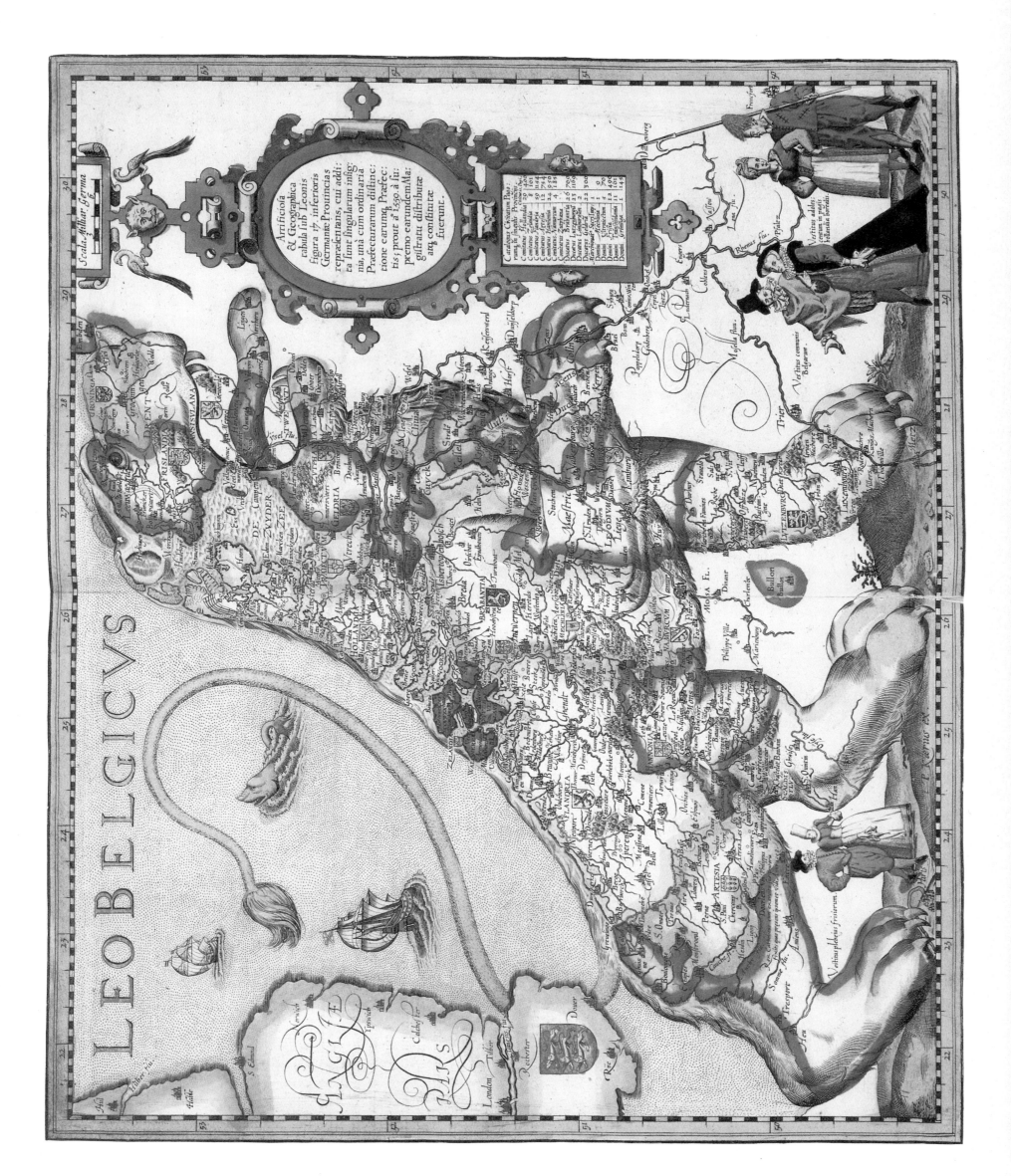

PLATE 12

Pieter van den Keere: Leo Belgicus

This wonderful cartographic curiosity – the Netherlands in the form of a Lion – was engraved by Pieter van den Keere in Amsterdam in 1617 and derived from an original design by Michael Aitzinger in 1583. Its success lay in part in the configuration of the land and in part from the fact that nearly all of the seventeen provinces of the ancient Netherlands incorporated a lion in their coat of arms. (Collection: British Library)

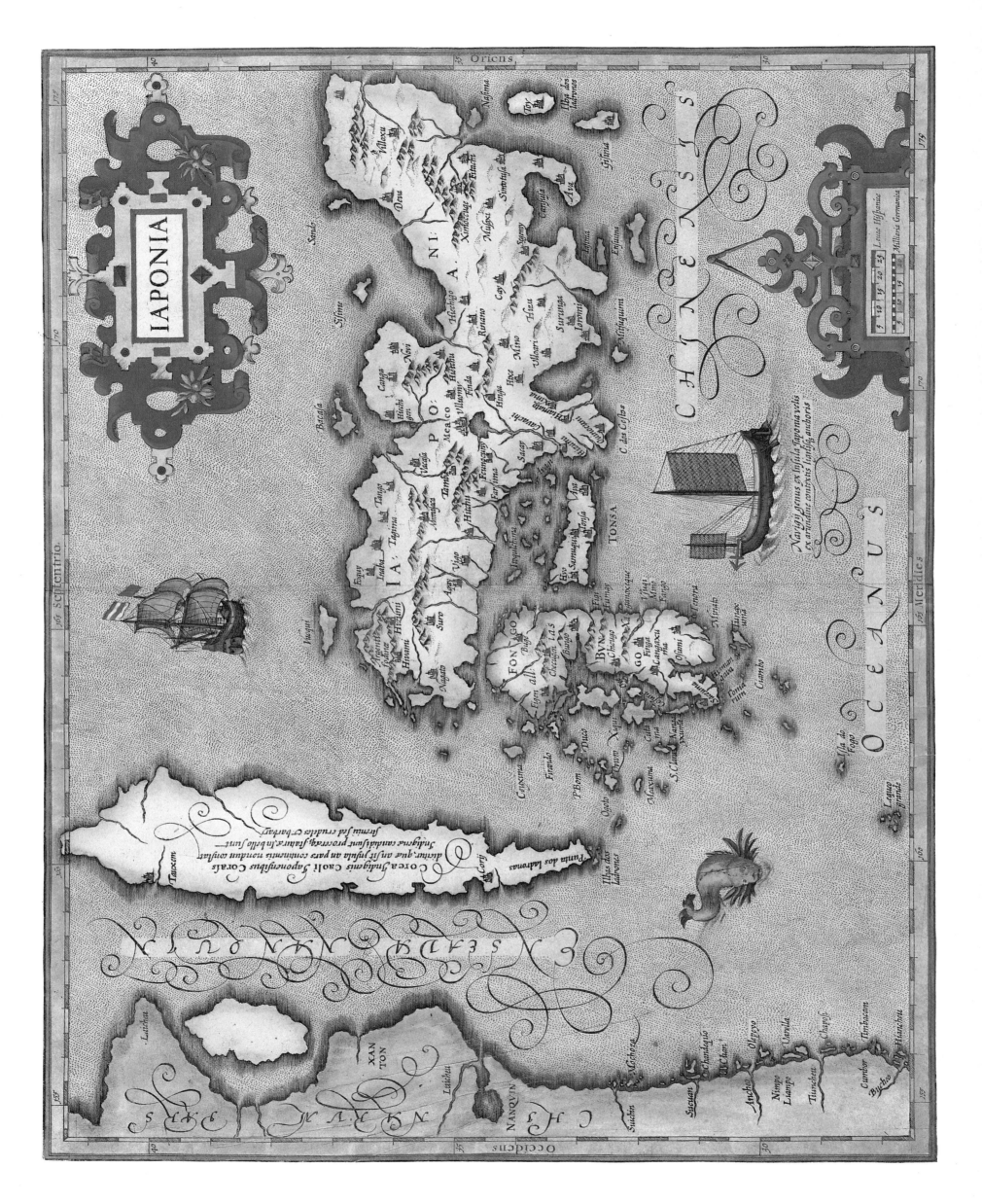

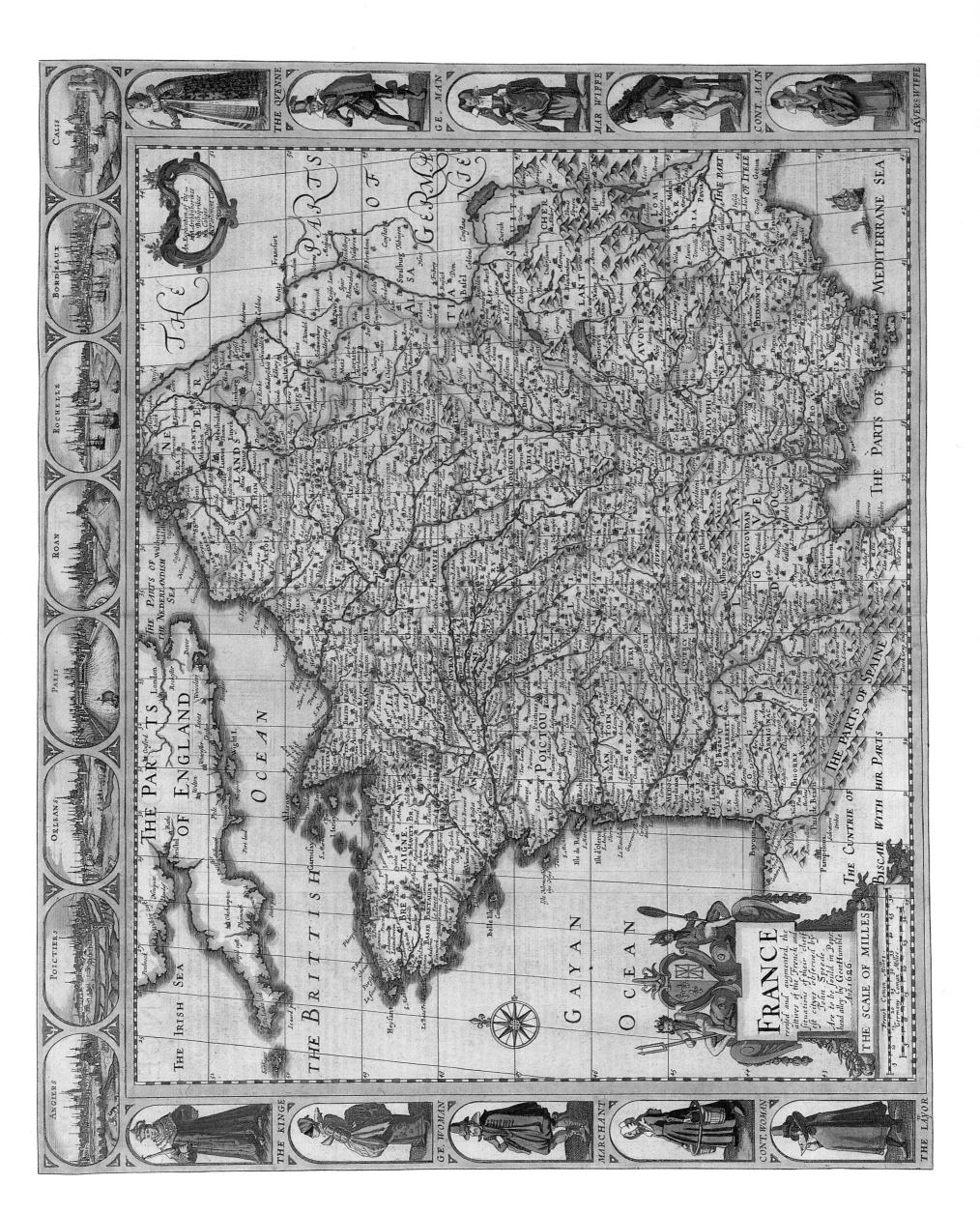

THE PARTS OF GERMANIE

THE PARTS OF THE NEDERLANDISH SEA

THE PARTS OF ENGLAND

OCEAN

THE IRISH SEA

THE BRITTISH SEA

GAYAN OCEAN

THE PARTS OF SPAINE

THE PARTS OF THE MEDITERRANE SEA

THE CUNTRIE OF BISCAIE WITH HIR PARTS

FRANCE
revised and augmented, the
aliures of the French and
situations of their chieff
est cityes observed by
John Speede.
Are to be sould in Popes
head alley by Geo: Humble.
Ano. 1626.

THE SCALE OF MILLES

PLATE 15

John Speed: France

The first world atlas by an Englishman, John Speed's Prospect of the Most Famous Parts of the World, *published in London in 1627, contained this beautiful map of France. Speed followed the Dutch model of a 'carte-à-figures', one of the most decorative of seventeenth-century map forms incorporating costumed figures and oval town views. (Collection: Jonathan Potter Ltd)*

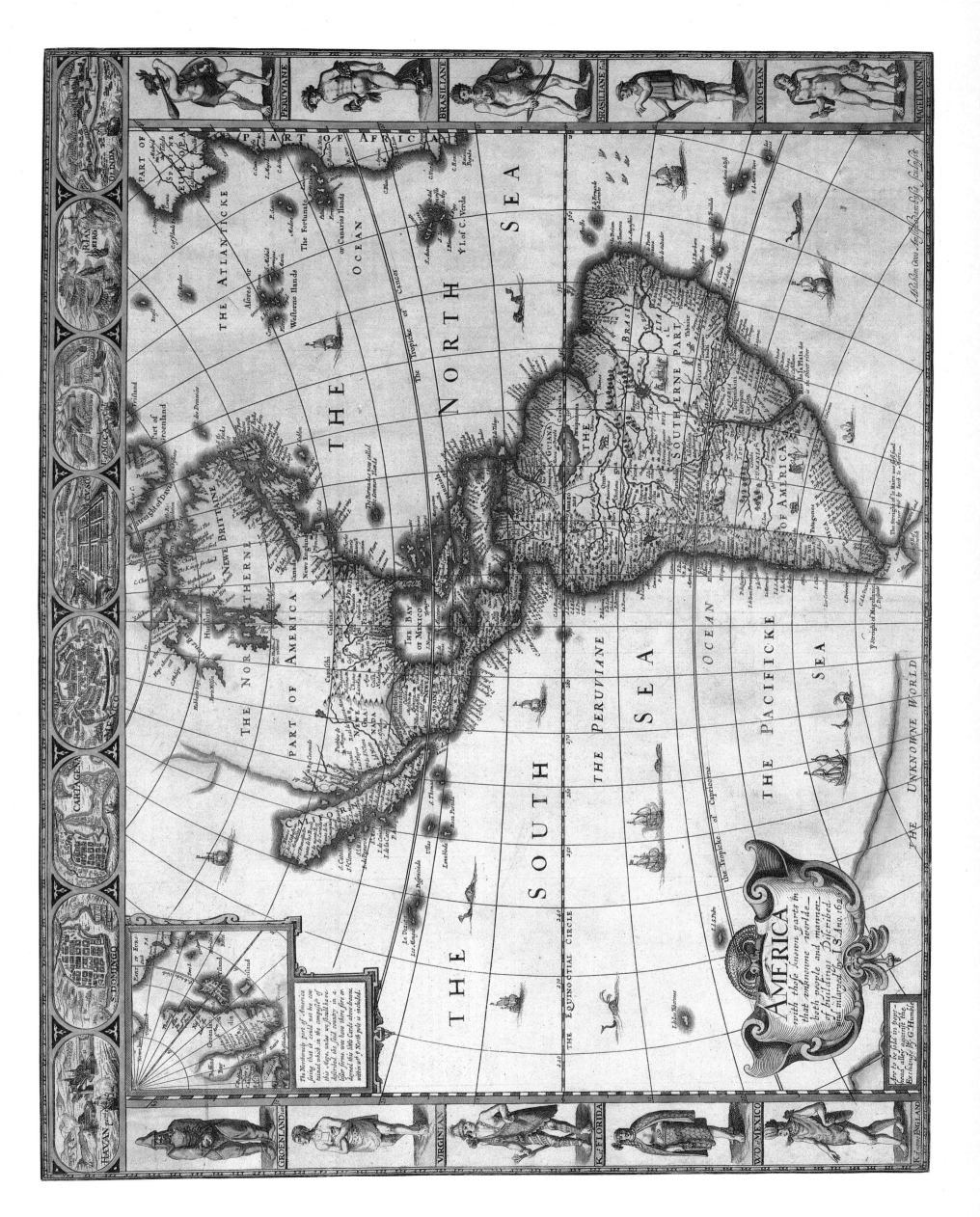

PLATE 16

John Speed: America

One of the finest early seventeenth-century maps of the New World, John Speed's America first appeared in London in 1627. John Speed was one of the earliest cartographers to propagate the theory of California as an island, perhaps one of the most amusing of cartographic misconceptions. (Collection: Jonathan Potter Ltd.)

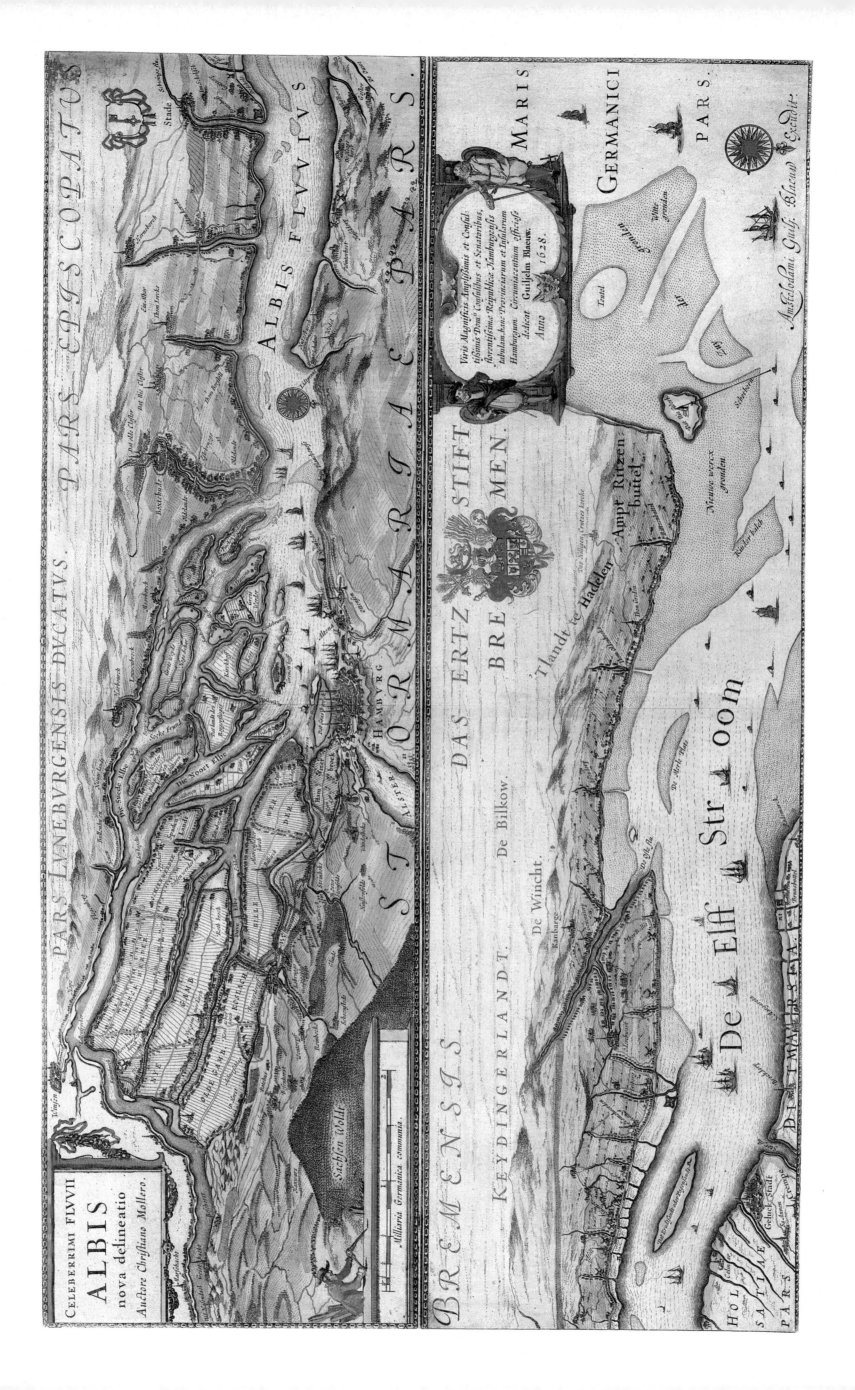

PLATE 17

Willem Blaeu: Celeberrimi Fluvii Albis

Willem Blaeu was the founder of one of the greatest Dutch mapmaking dynasties of the seventeenth century. This map appeared in one of his earliest world atlases, the Atlas Appendix *(Amsterdam, 1630) and depicts almost in bird's eye perspective, and on two tiers, the famous North German river, the Elbe, and the thriving Hanseatic port of Hamburg. (Collection: Jonathan Potter Ltd.)*

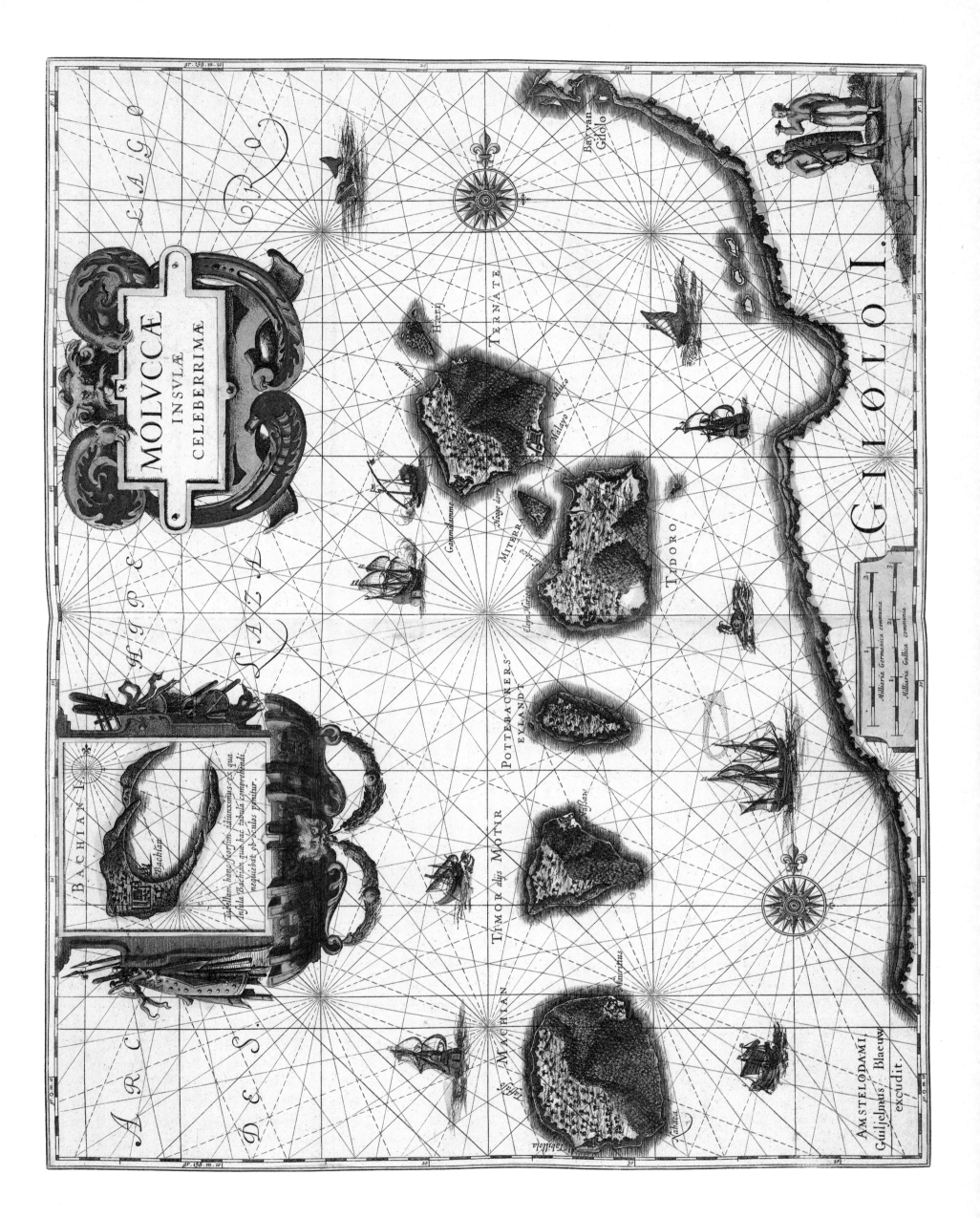

MOLVCCÆ
INSVLÆ
CELEBERRIMÆ

GILOLOI.

Bayvan
Gilolo

TERNATE

TIDORO

POTTEBACKERS
EYLANDT

TIMOR alijs MOTIR

MACHIAN

BACHIAN

Bachian

Tabellam hanc, seorsim adiunximus ex qua
insula Bachian quæ hac tabula comprehendi
nequibat ob oculos ponitur.

AMSTELODAMI,
Guiljelmus Blaeuw
excudit.

PLATE 18

Willem Blaeu: Molluccae Insulae Celeberrimae

Willem Blaeu's early representation of the Spice Islands reflects growing Dutch influence and interest in South East Asia following the establishment of the Dutch East India Company in 1602. Blaeu's map depicts an array of island forts and trading posts off the west coast of Gilolo, the largest of the Molucca Islands. It was first published in Amsterdam in 1630. (Collection: British Library)

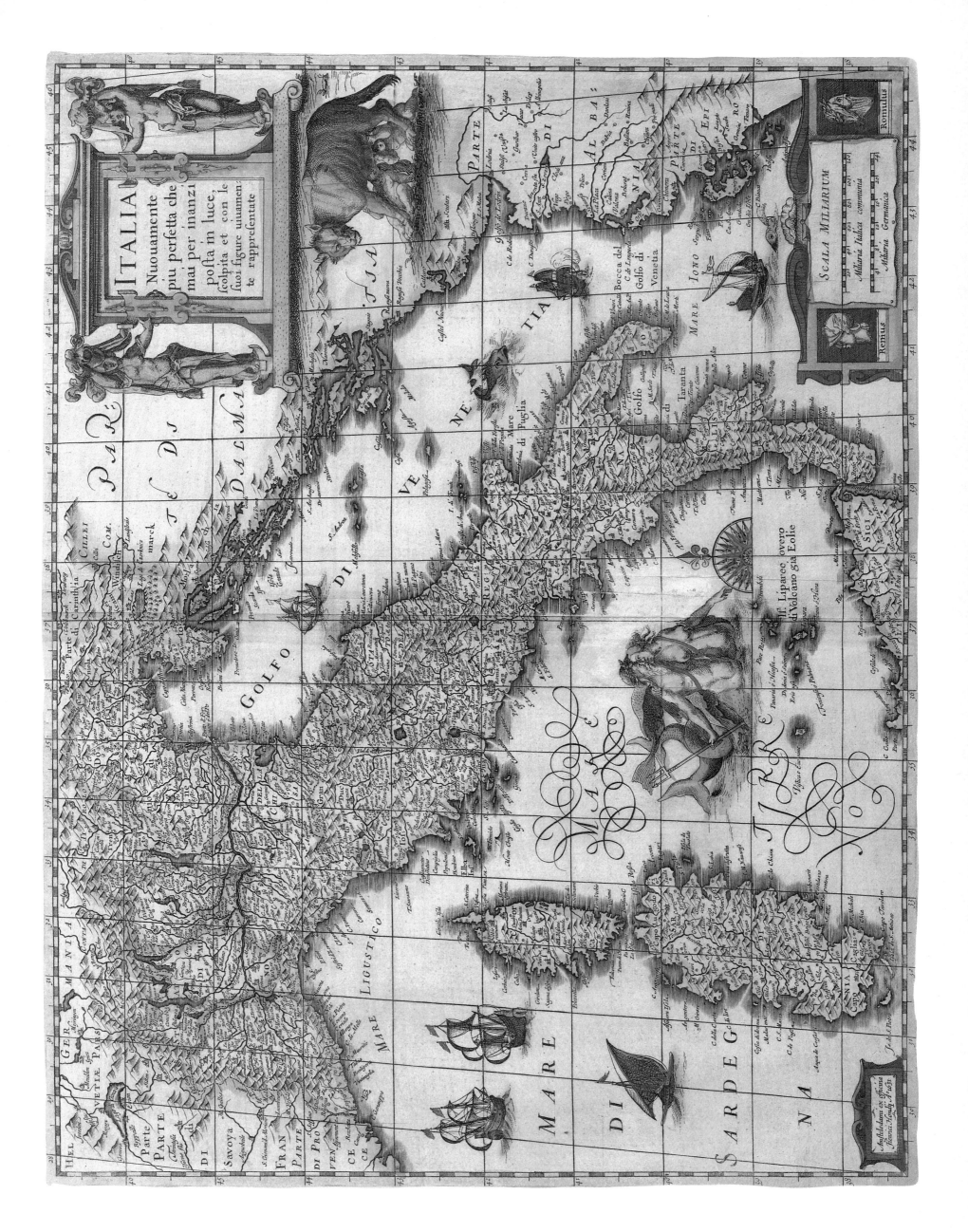

ITALIA Nuouamente piu perfetta che mai per inanzi posta in luce, scolpita et con le suoi figure uiuamente rapprefentate

SCALA MILLIARIUM

Romulus

Remus

PLATE 19

Henricus Hondius: Italia

Henricus Hondius' refined and beautifully designed map of Italy harks back to her classical roots in the now familiar images of Romulus and Remus and the she-wolf. One of a series of new maps by Henricus first published in 1631, it was part of a concerted attempt to rival the great map publications of the Blaeu family. (Collection: Jonathan Potter Ltd.)

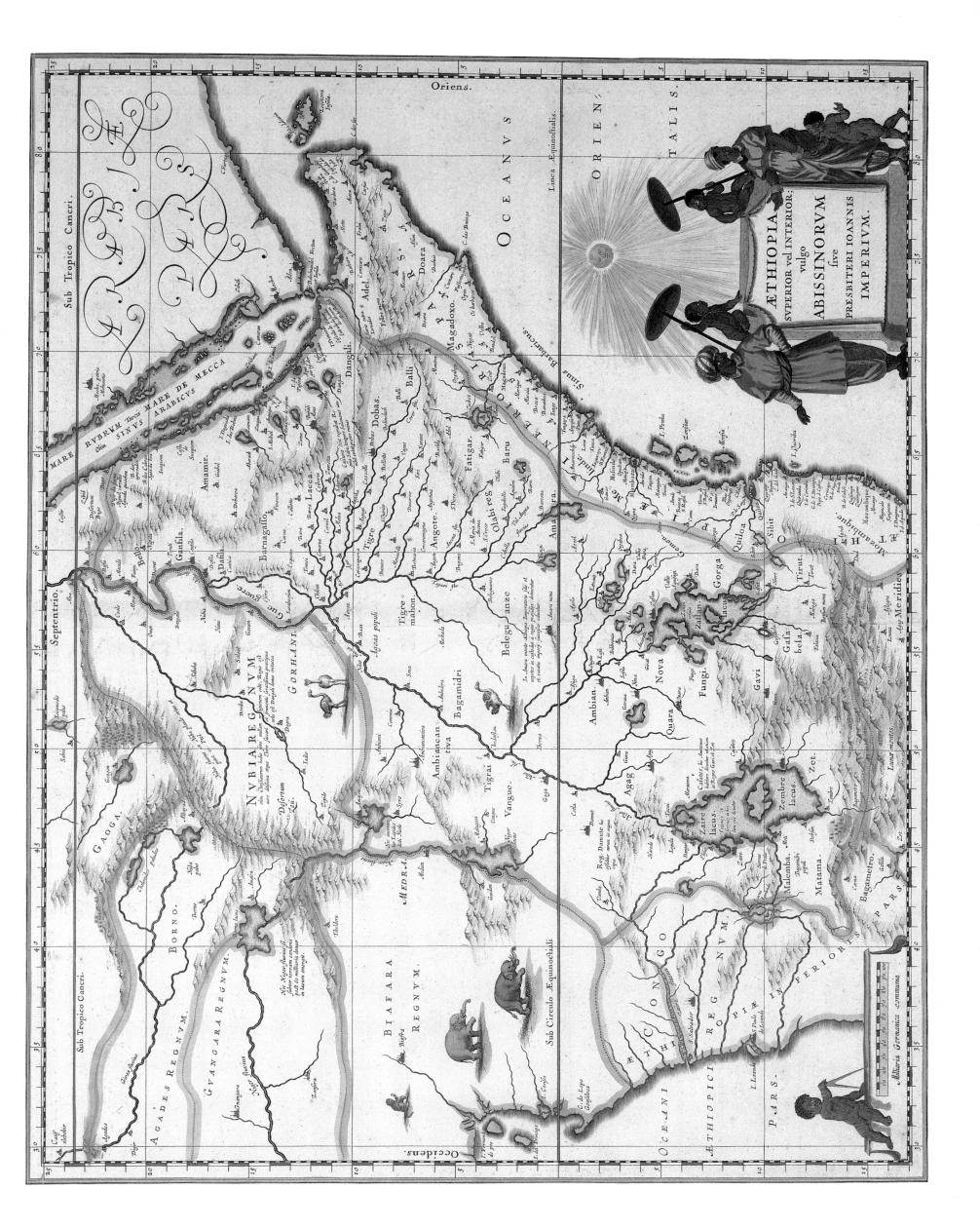

Oriens.

OCEANVS

Linea Æquinoctialis.

ORIEN—

—TALIS.

ÆTHIOPIA SVPERIOR vel INTERIOR; vulgo ABISSINORVM sive PRESBITERI IOANNIS IMPERIVM.

Sub Tropico Cancri.

ARABIÆ PARS

MARE RVBRVM Turcis MARE DE MECCA Olim. SINVS ARABICVS

Septentrio.

Sub Tropico Cancri.

NVBIA REGNVM

GORHANI.

GAOGA.

BORNO.

AGADES REGNVM.

GVANGARA REGNVM.

MEDRA.

BIAFARA REGNVM.

Sub Circulo Equinoctiali.

ÆTHIOPICI REGNVM.

ÆTHIOPIÆ INFERIORIS PARS.

ÆCONGO

OCEANI ÆTHIOPICI PARS.

Occidens.

Sinus Barbaricus

Amara.

Tigre.

Angote.

Olabieg.

Baru.

Fatigar.

Dobas.

Balli.

Magadoxo.

Adel.

Doara.

Dangali.

Amamir.

Bello.

Ginfila.

Barnagaſſo.

Ambiancan tiva.

Tigrai

Vangue.

Belegu anze.

Bagamidri.

Ambian.

Agag.

Zet.

Nova.

Quara.

Fungi.

Gorga.

Zaflan. lacus

Gafa bela.

Gavi.

Tirut.

Sibit.

Quiloa.

Melinda

Mombaza.

Zembre lacus.

Zaire lacus.

Malemba.

Matama.

Bagametro.

Luna montes.

Guangue Bnoco.

Tigre mahon.

Agoas populi.

Milliaria Germanica communia.

Joan Blaeu: Aethiopia Superior vel Interior

Joan Blaeu's beautiful map of Central Africa, first published in Amsterdam in 1635, is one of the last maps to give credence to the fabled kingdom of Prester John. Since the time of the Crusades it was believed that somewhere in India or Africa existed a powerful Christian potentate who might assist Europe in its war against Islam. The search proved in vain but it provides one of the most interesting and enduring survivals of medieval fable. (Collection: Jonathan Potter Ltd.)

ASIA
noviter delineata
Auctore
Guiljelmo Blaeuw.

PLATE 22

Willem Blaeu: Asia

The wonders of the Orient are given free rein in this beautifully designed and engraved 'carte-à-figures' first published by Willem Blaeu in Amsterdam in about 1618 and incorporated almost unchanged into the magnificent Blaeu atlases of the next fifty years. (Collection: Jonathan Potter Ltd.)

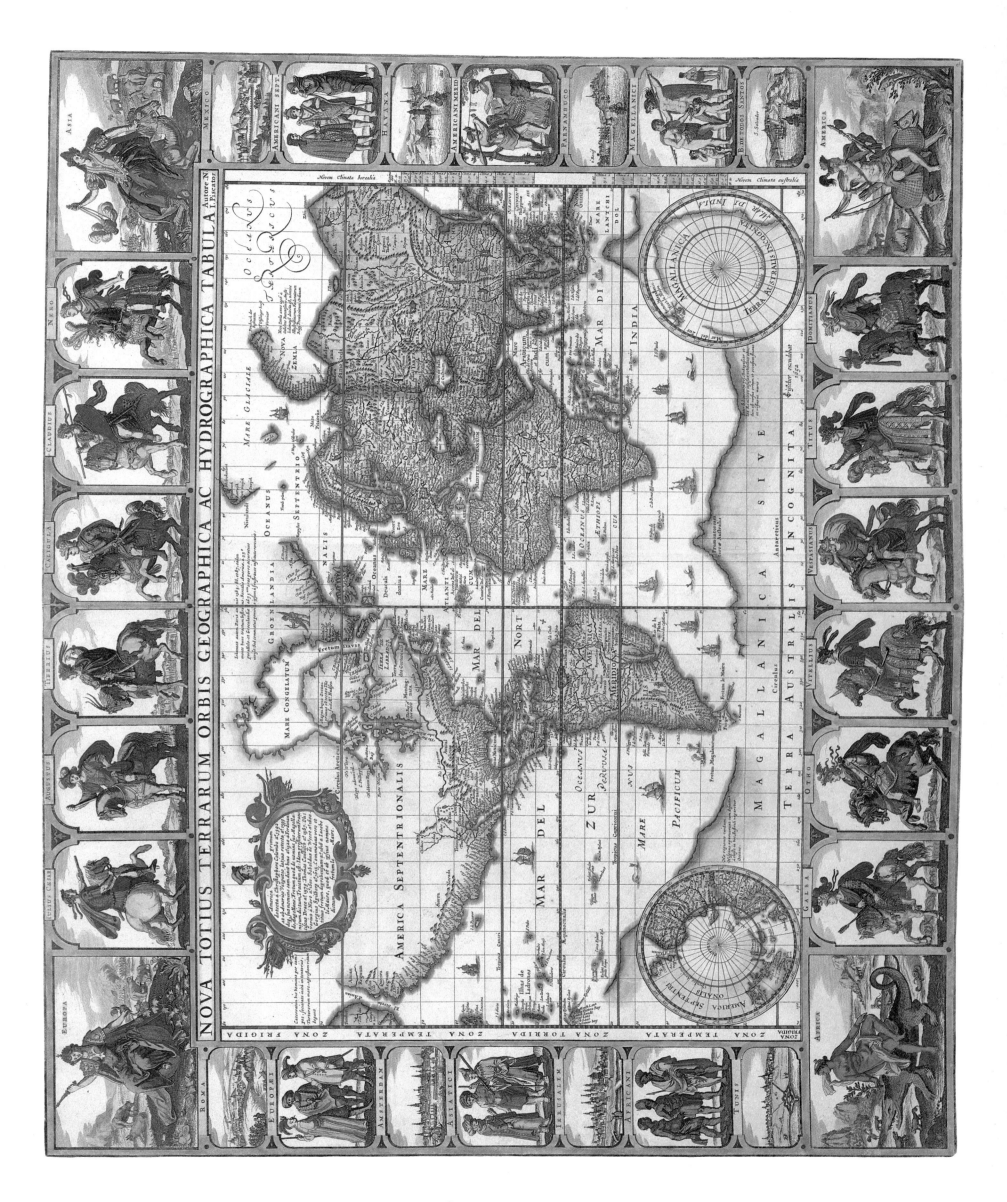

NOVA TOTIUS TERRARUM ORBIS GEOGRAPHICA AC HYDROGRAPHICA TABULA Autore N. I. Piscator.

Andreas Cellarius: Coeli Stellati Christiani Haemis-
phaerium

This beautifully decorative chart from Andreas Cellarius' Atlas
Coelestis *is modelled on the work of Julius Schiller of Augsburg
and represents an attempt by scholars of the period to
Christianize the heavens. In an age of religious wars, the
heavens were to become a Bible in the Sky and we are presented
with images of the Old and New Testament in place of the
traditional constellations. (Collection: Jonathan Potter Ltd.)*

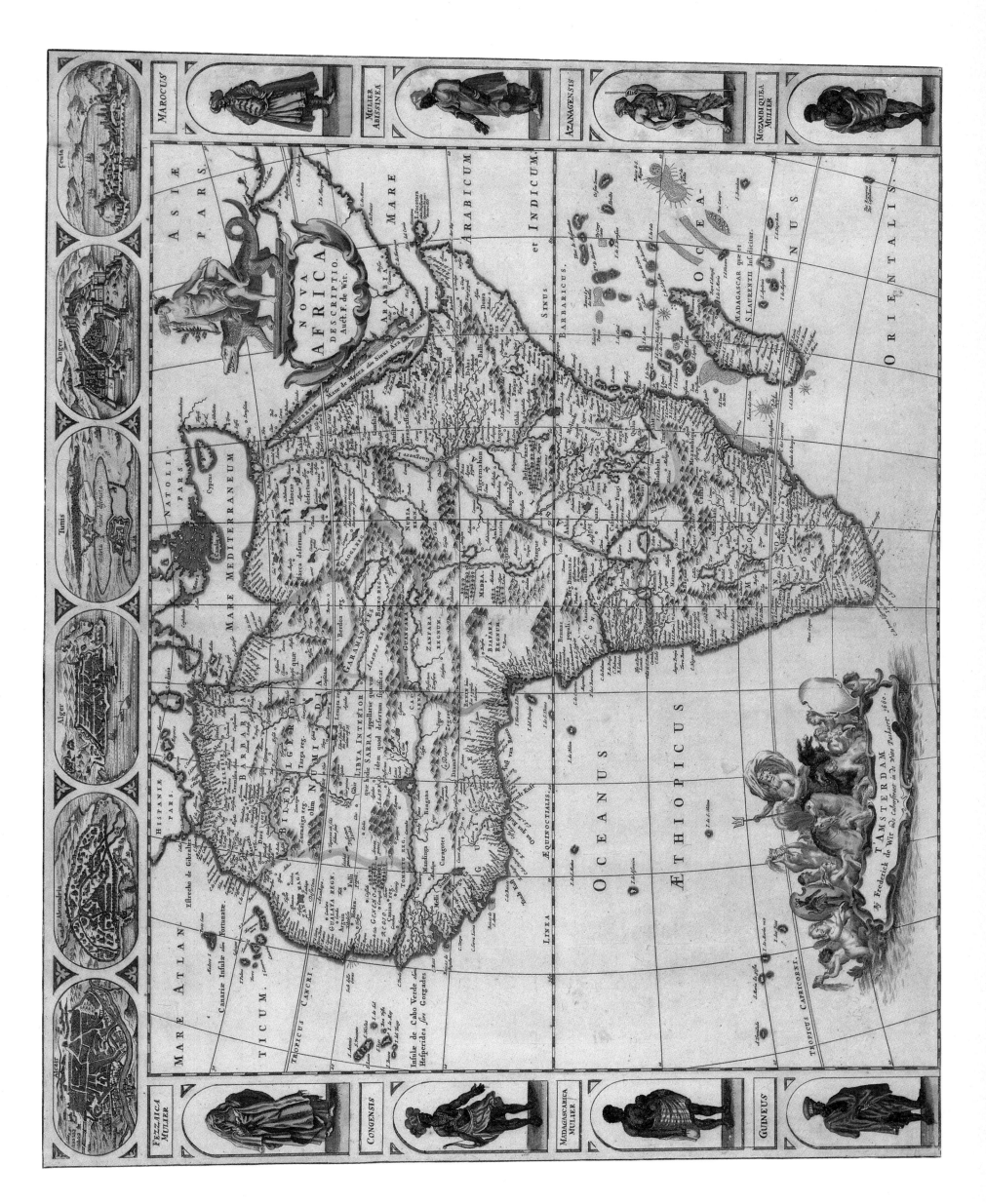

PLATE 25

Frederick de Wit: Africa

Frederick de Wit's uncommon 'carte-à-figures', Africa first appeared in Amsterdam in 1660 continuing the great tradition of Dutch mapmaking established by Blaeu, Jansson and Hondius. (Collection: Jonathan Potter Ltd.)

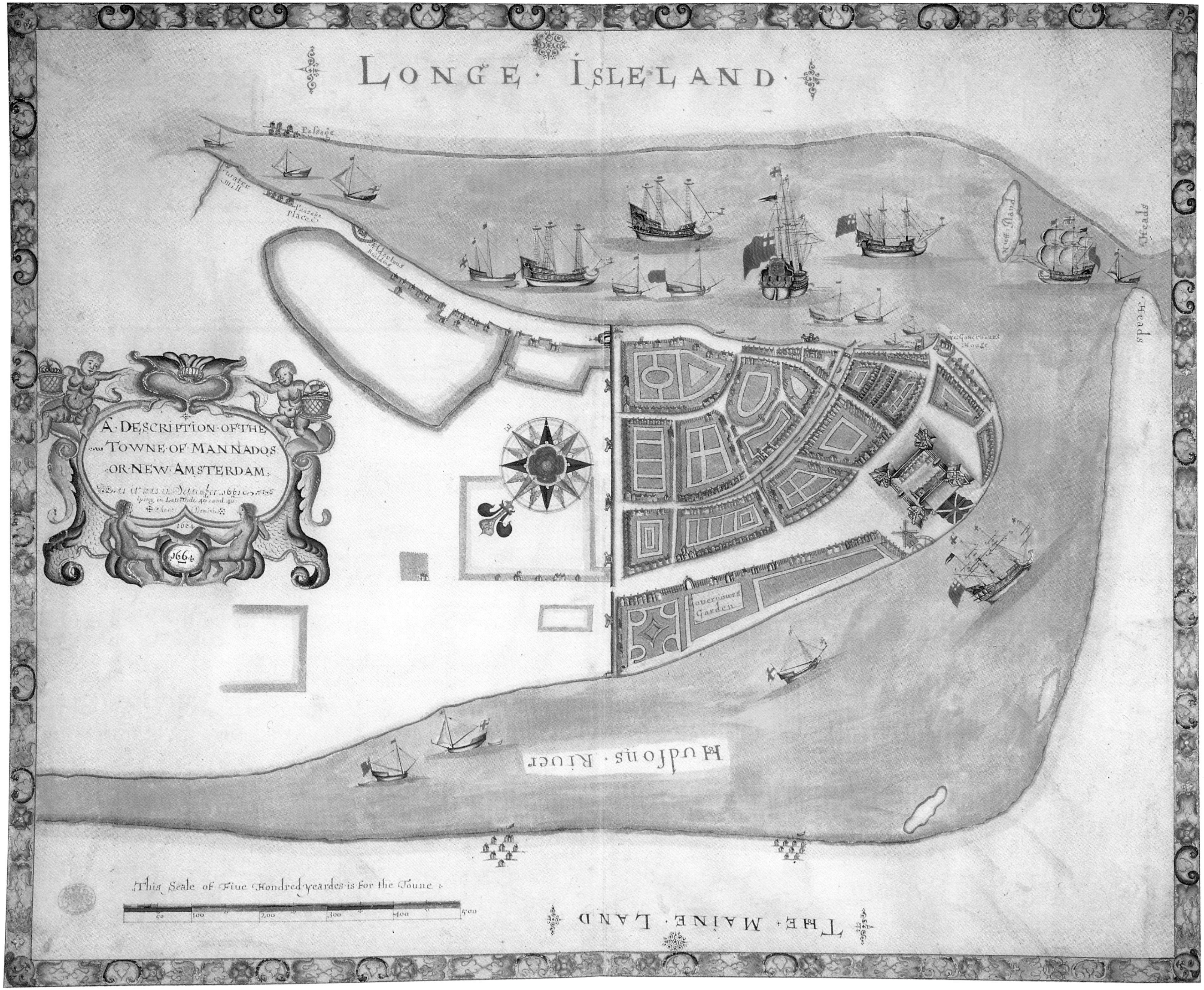
LONGE · ISLELAND
A · DESCRIPTION · OF THE
TOWNE · OF · MANNADOS
OR · NEW · AMSTERDAM
as it was in September 1661
lying in Latitude 40 and 40
Anno Domini
1664
Water Mill
Passage Place
Passage
Nutt Iland
Heads
Heads
Governours Garden
Hudsons · River
This Scale of Fiue Hondred yeardes is for the Toune
50
100
200
300
400
500
THE · MAINE · LAND

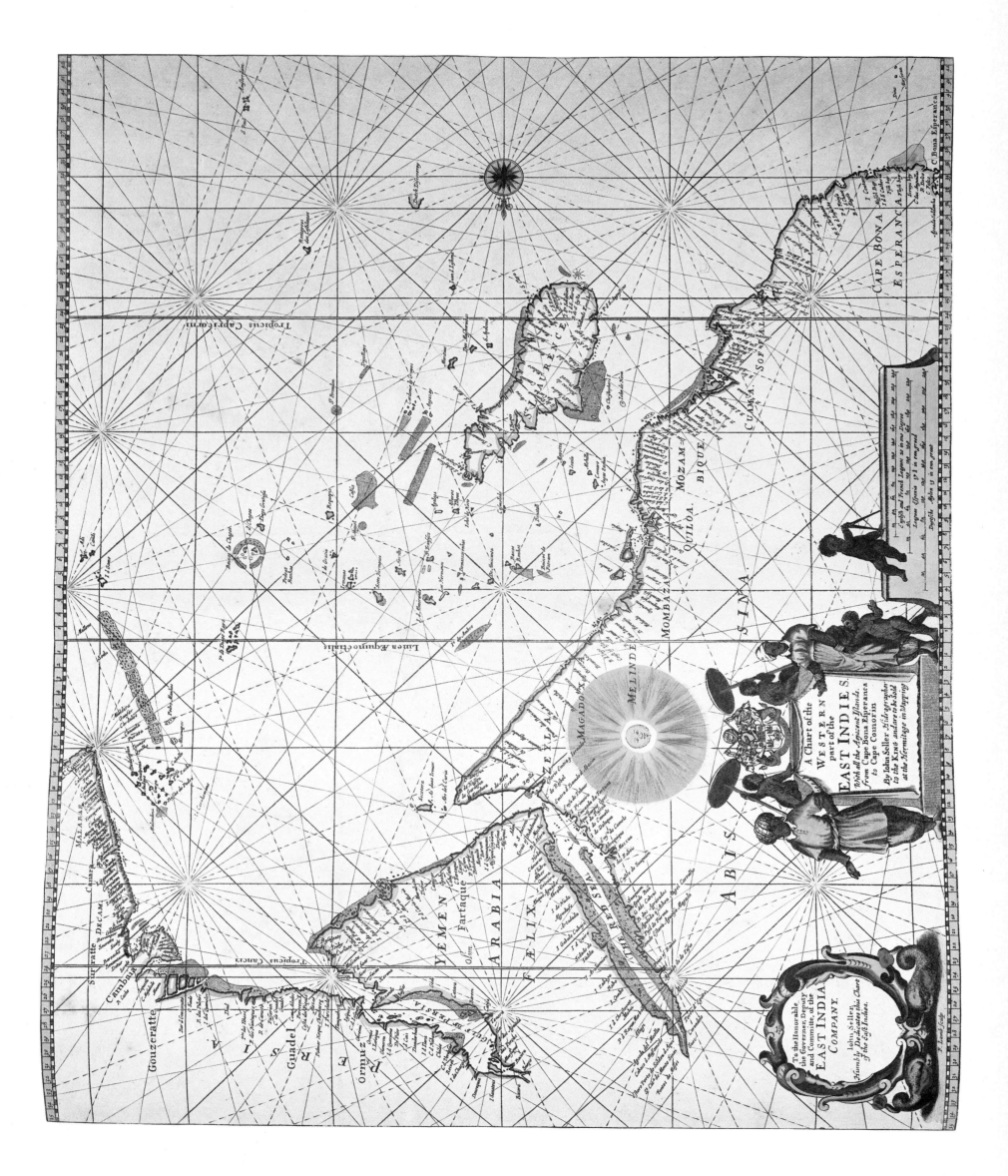

PLATE 28

John Seller: A Chart of the Western Part of the East
Indies

*A landmark in the history of English chartmaking, John
Seller's* Atlas Maritimus *or Sea Atlas published in London in
1675, from which this chart is taken, was one of the first great
English maritime atlases and exposed the reliance of most
seventeenth-century navigators on charts produced in the
Netherlands. Seller was no exception, the cartouche is lifted
directly from Blaeu's map of East Africa and many of his charts
were reworkings of copperplates which he had himself purchased
in the Netherlands. (Collection: British Library)*

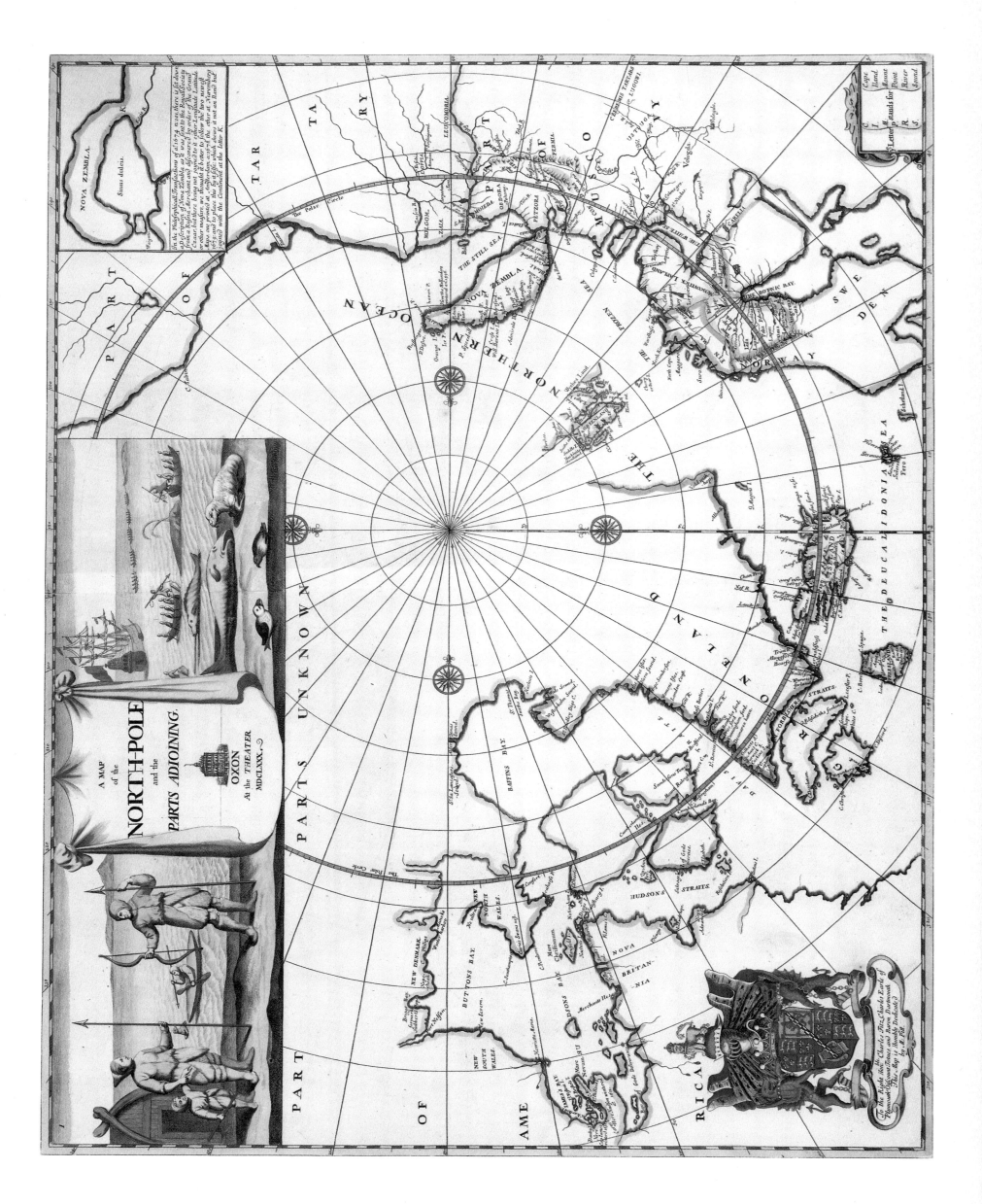

A MAP
of the
NORTH-POLE
and the
PARTS ADIOINING.

OXON
At the THEATER
MDCLXXX.

To the Right Hon.ble Charles Fitz Charles Earle of
Plymouth, Vicount Totnes, and Baron Dartmouth.
This Map is humbly Dedicate.d
by A. Pitt.

NOVA ZEMBLA

Sinus dulcis.

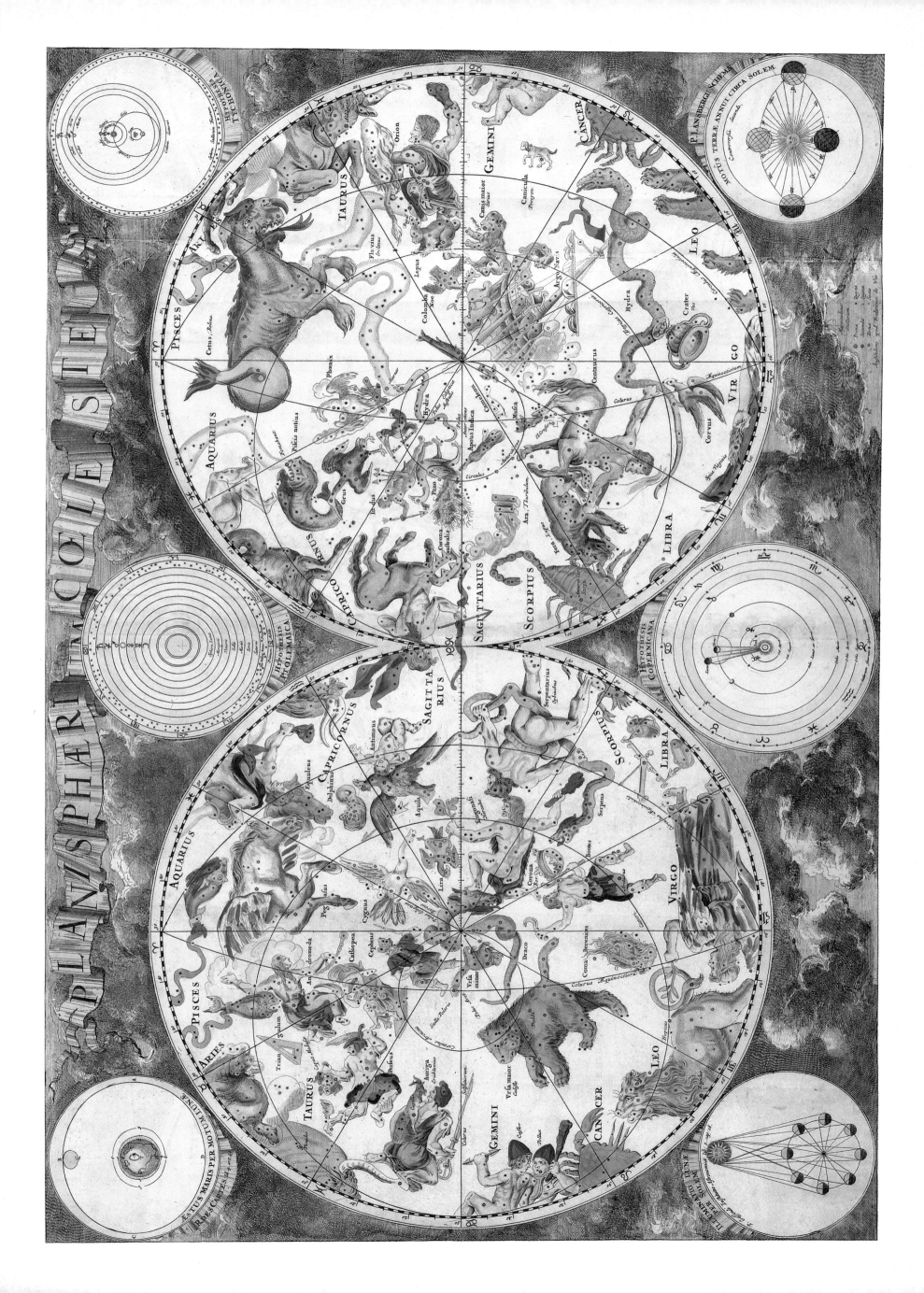

PLATE 30

Frederick de Wit: Planisphaeri Coeleste

Frederick de Wit's refined map production was not confined to the World; this spectacular map of the Heavens was published in 1680 and shows the northern and southern hemispheres with traditional representations of the constellations and signs of the Zodiac. (Collection: Jonathan Potter Ltd.)

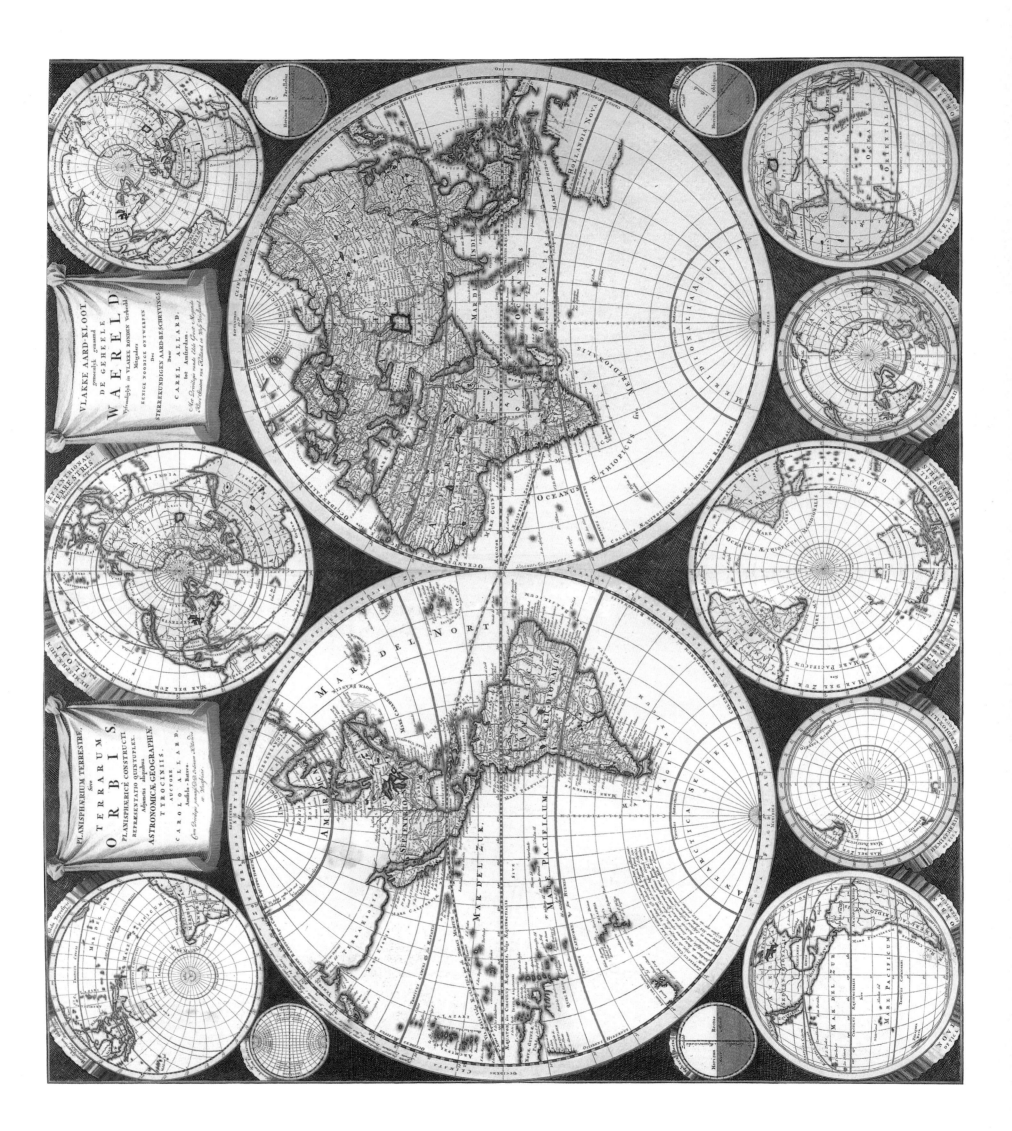

PLATE 31

Carel Allard: Planisphaerium Terrestre

A striking double hemisphere world map by Carel Allard, contrasting quite markedly with the traditional decorative embellishment of other Dutch maps of the period. The array of hemispheres and the dark cross-hatched engraving of the background makes this one of the most unusual and eye-catching world maps of the late seventeenth century (Amsterdam, 1696). (Collection: Jonathan Potter Ltd.)

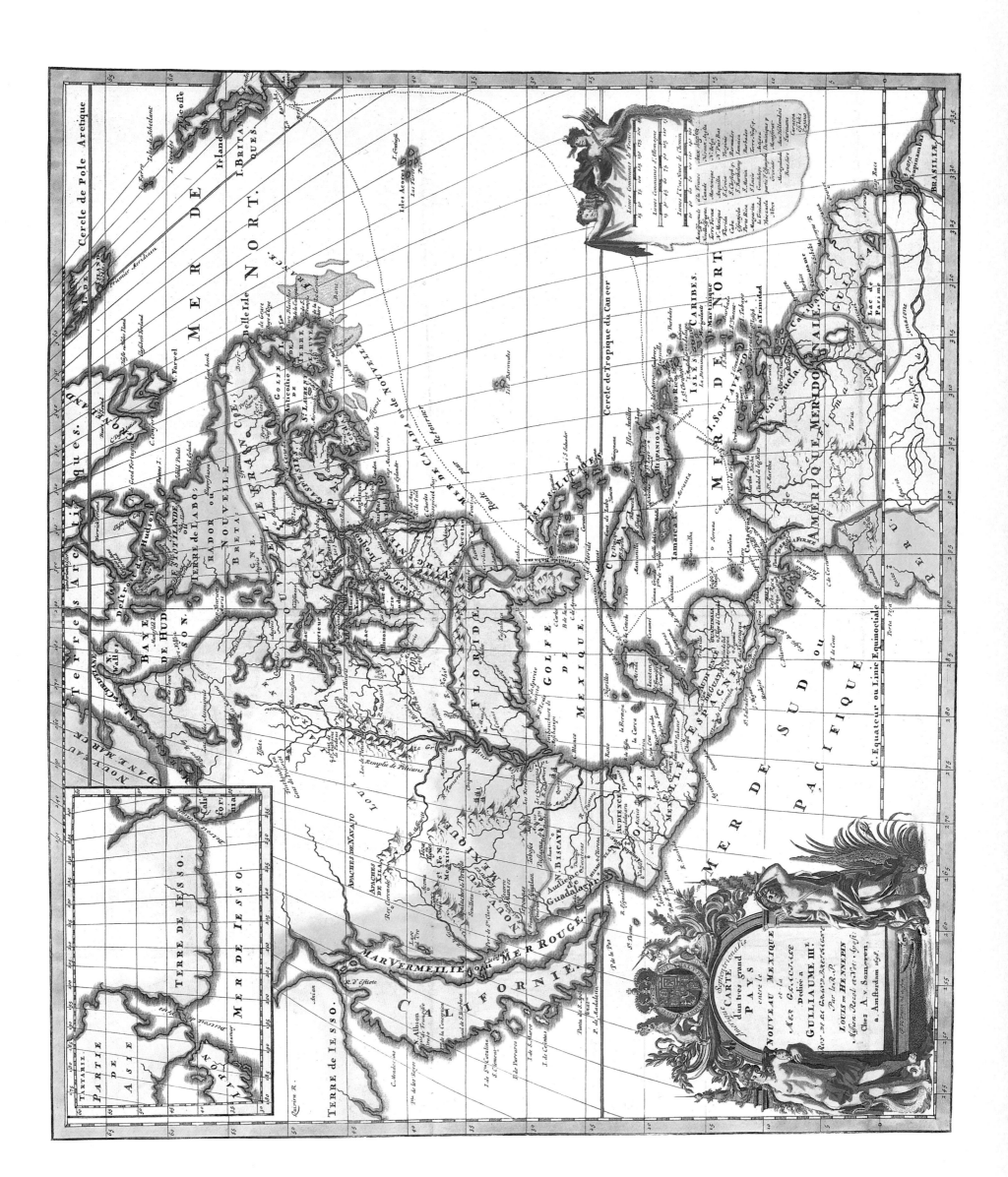

PLATE 32

Louis Hennepin: Amerique Septentrionale

*A beautifully designed and uncommon map of North America
(Amsterdam, 1698). Father Louis Hennepin, a Belgian priest,
was one of the earliest Europeans to explore the Upper
Mississippi and this map accompanied the account of his treks.
One of the most prominent features is the continued credence given
to the theory of California as an island, an idea that persisted
for another fifty years. (Collection: Jonathan Potter Ltd.)*

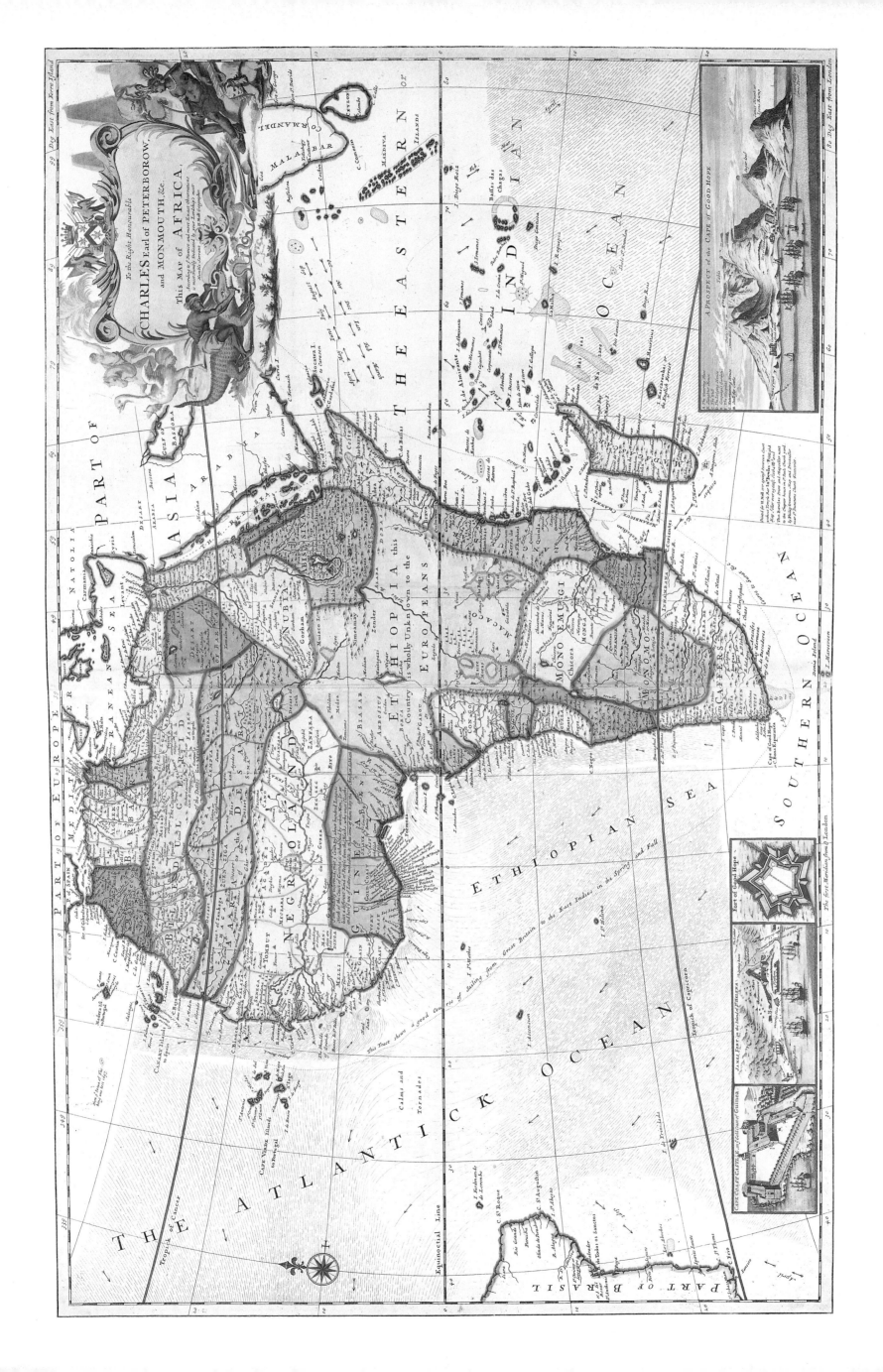

PLATE 33

Herman Moll: Africa

Herman Moll, a German emigré, was one of the most outspoken and opinionated English mapmakers of the early eighteenth century. First published in 1710, this wonderful map of the continent of Africa combines a wealth of detail and information with charming vignettes of strategic ports of call around the African coastline. (Collection: Jonathan Potter Ltd.)

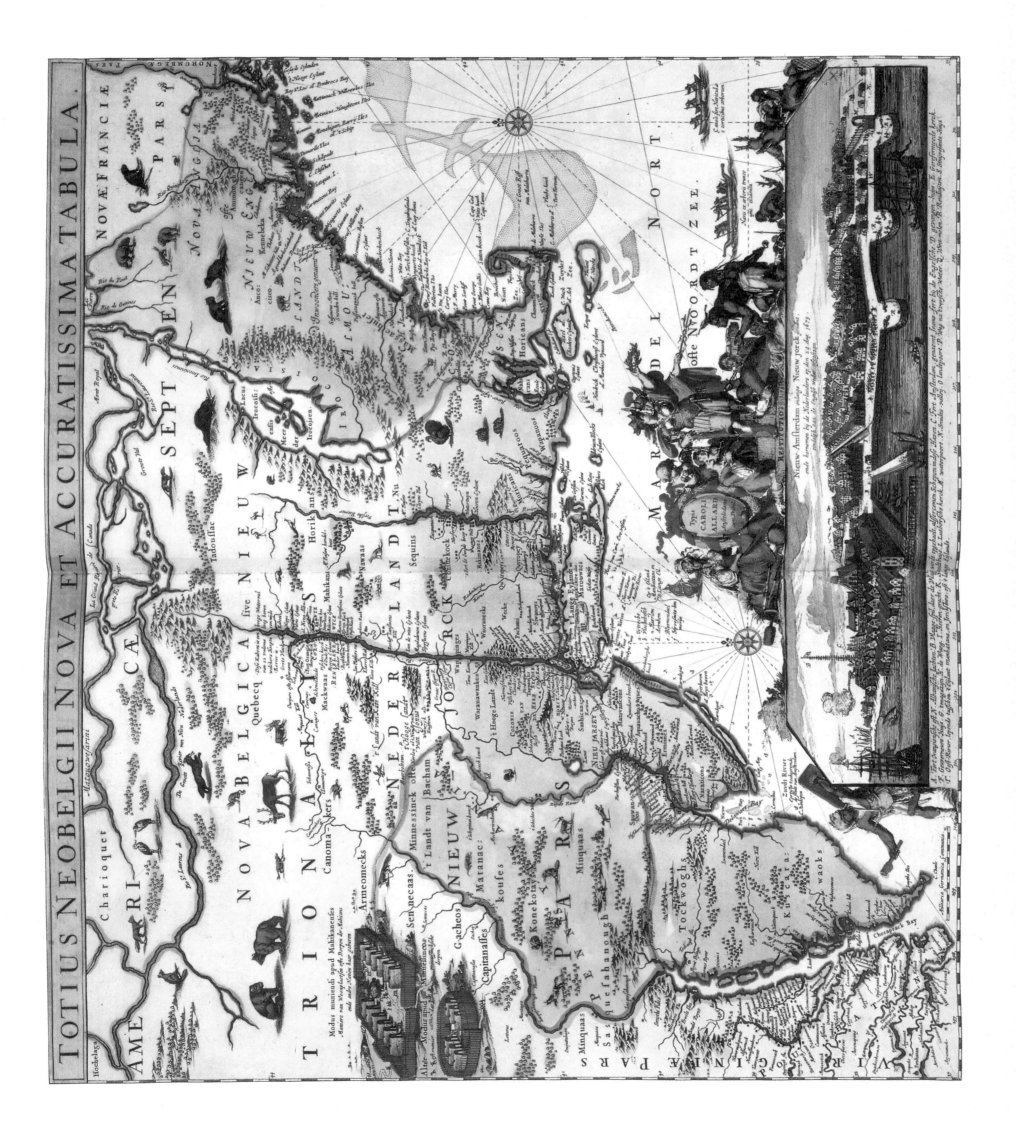

PLATE 34

Carel Allard: Totius Neo Belgii Nova et Accuratissima Tabula

One of the most famous images of late seventeenth-century New England, this wonderful map of the East Coast by Carel Allard incorporates the so-called 'Restituo' view of New Amsterdam celebrating the Dutch recapture of the town in 1673. Earlier images of the town based on Nicolas Visscher had shown a quiet pastoral settlement. The image here is one of violence and military action portrayed in the tableaux of smoking cannons and marching soldiers (Amsterdam, c.1700). (Collection: British Library)

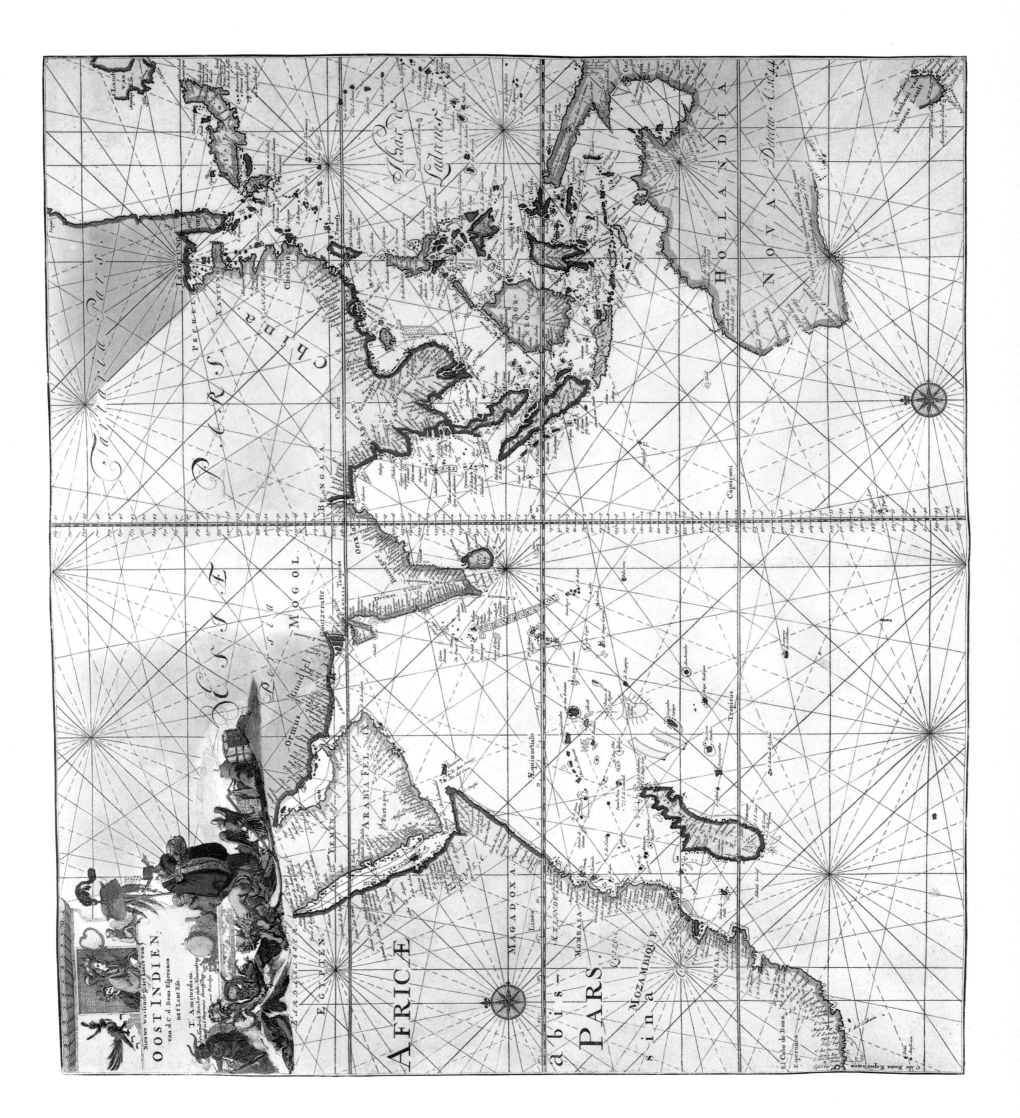

PLATE 35

Hendrick Doncker: Oost Indien

Hendrick Doncker's beautiful chart of the Indian Ocean is one of the many Dutch maps to show the extent of European knowledge of Australia prior to the voyages of Pacific exploration in the late eighteenth century. An important chart for the vessels of the Dutch East India Company on their route from the Cape of Good Hope to Batavia, it was first published in Amsterdam in 1705. (Collection: Jonathan Potter Ltd)

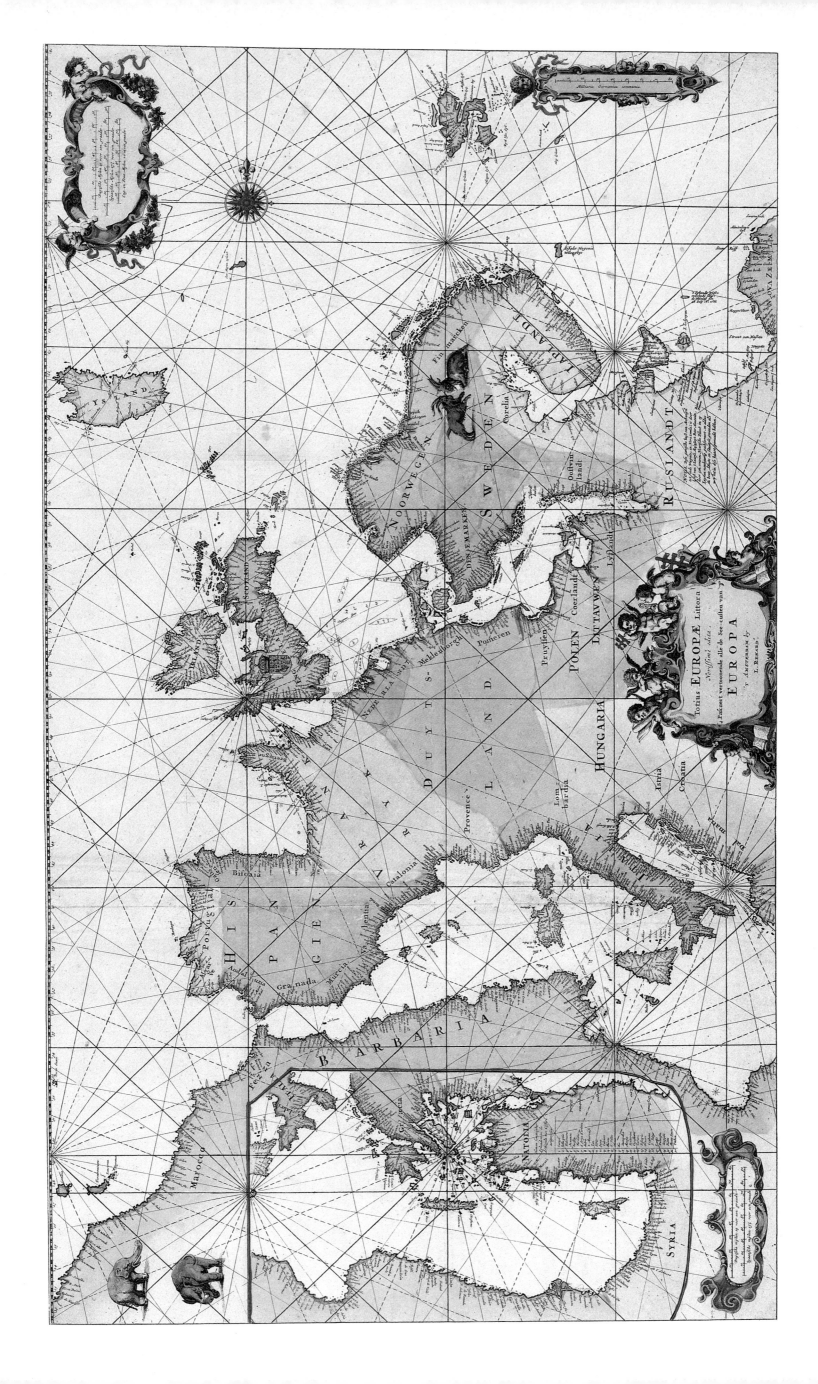

PLATE 36

Louis Renard: Totius Europae Littorae

One of the most decorative Dutch charts of the coasts of Europe, issued in Amsterdam by Louis Renard (in 1715). Its unusual orientation and striking original colours are complemented by interesting animal vignettes and decoratively designed cartouches. (Collection: Jonathan Potter Ltd.)

Dighton del.

Geography Bewitched!
or, a droll Caricature MAP of SCOTLAND.

London.Printed for Bowles & Carver. No.69.St.Pauls Church Yard. 4 June 1794.

Dighton del.

Geography Bewitched!
or; a droll Caricature MAP of ENGLAND and WALES.

London.Printed for Bowles & Carver . No.69.St. Pauls Church Yard.

PLATE 37

Bowles and Carver: Geography Bewitched

The ability of maps to amuse as well as inform is clearly demonstrated by this charming pair of caricature maps of England and Wales, and Scotland, which were published by Bowles and Carver (London, 1794). National characteristics are quite clearly drawn – the English penchant for beer and the Scottish love of tartan! (Collection: Jonathan Potter Ltd.)

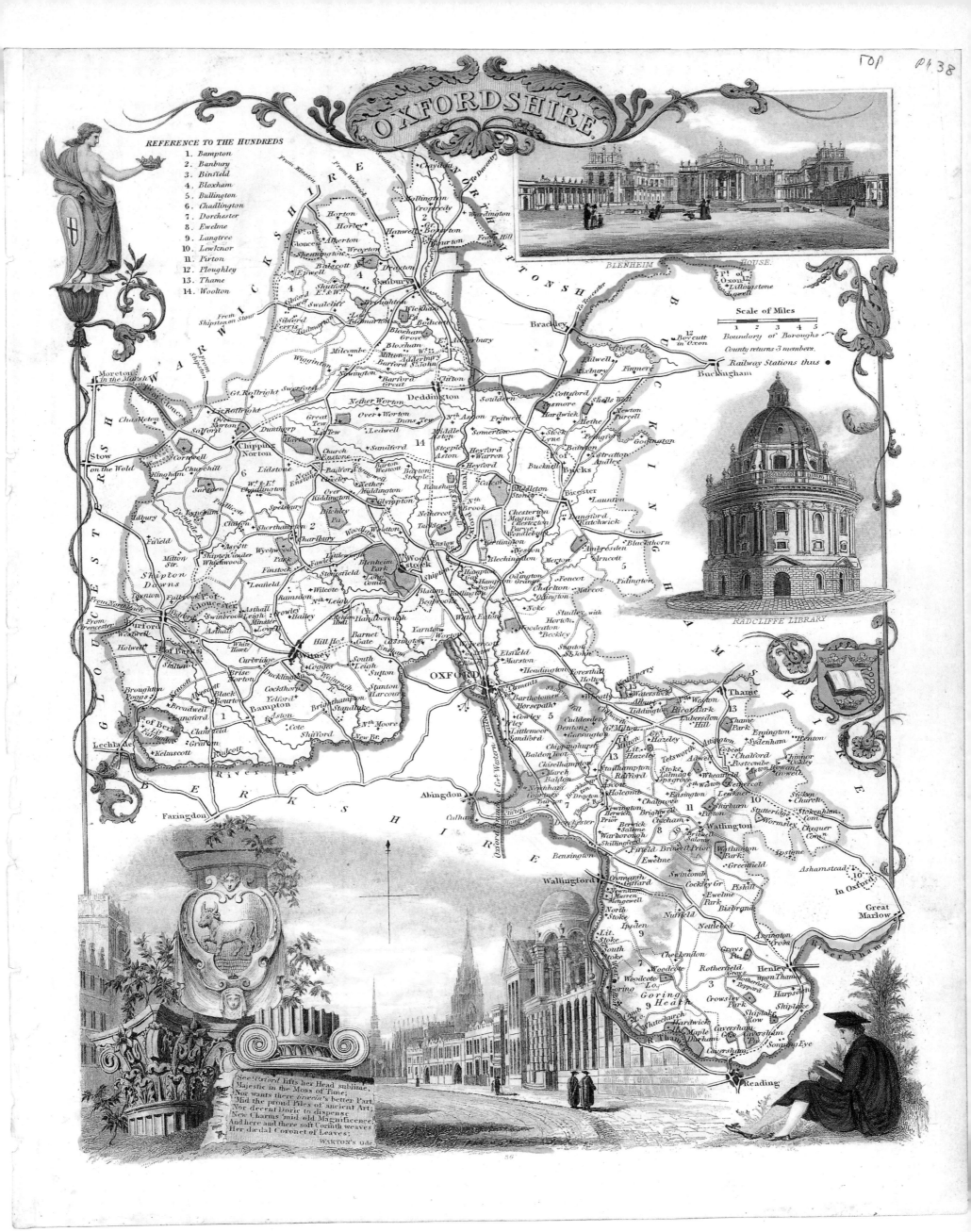

OXFORDSHIRE.

REFERENCE TO THE HUNDREDS

1. Bampton
2. Banbury
3. Binfield
4. Bloxham
5. Bullington
6. Chadlington
7. Dorchester
8. Ewelme
9. Langtree
10. Lewknor
11. Pirton
12. Ploughley
13. Thame
14. Woolton

BLENHEIM HOUSE.

RADCLIFFE LIBRARY

Scale of Miles

Boundary of Boroughs
County returns 3 members.
Railway Stations thus

See Oxford lifts her Head sublime,
Majestic in the Moss of Time;
Nor wants there Genius's better Part,
Mid the proud Piles of ancient Art,
Nor decent Doric to dispense
New Charms 'mid old Magnificence
And here and there soft Corinth weaves
Her dædal Coronet of Leaves.

WARTON's Ode.

PLATE 38

Thomas Moule: Oxfordshire

Thomas Moule's English Counties Delineated *(London, 1836) is one of the most sought-after of early nineteenth-century English county atlases. Moule, an antiquary and heraldic scholar, embellished his maps with beautiful vignettes and heraldic devices that draw comparison with their seventeenth-century predecessors. This charming map of the University County of Oxfordshire incorporates elements still quite recognizable today. (Private Collection)*

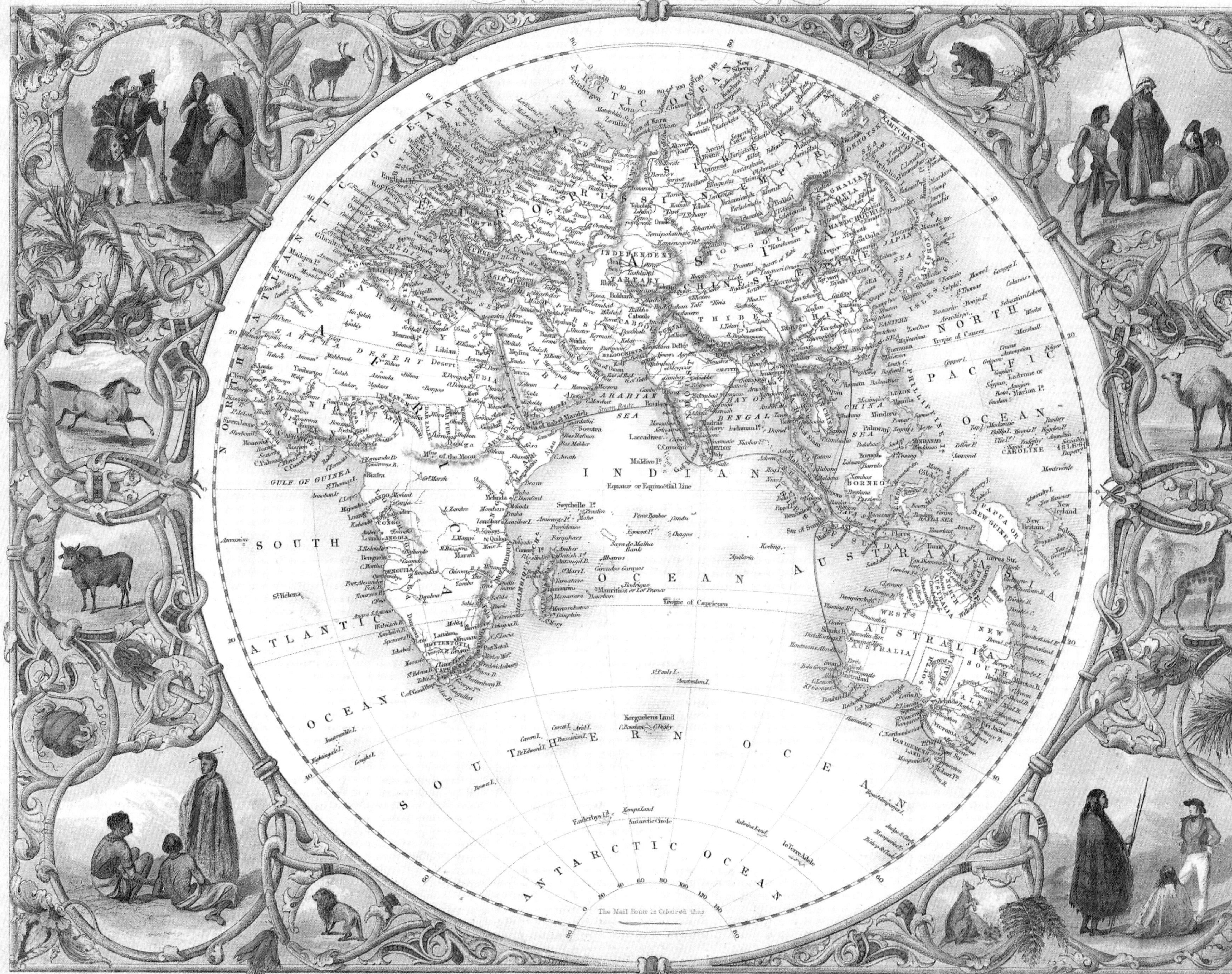

EASTERN HEMISPHERE.

JOHN TALLIS & COMPANY, LONDON & NEW YORK.

The Map, Drawn & Engraved by J. Rapkin.

Drawn & Engraved by J. Rogers.

ARCTIC OCEAN

NORTH PACIFIC OCEAN

INDIAN OCEAN

AUSTRALIA

SOUTH AUSTRALIA

WEST AUSTRALIA

NORTH AUSTRALIA

NEW SOUTH WALES

AFRICA

DESERT OF SAHARA

GULF OF GUINEA

SOUTH ATLANTIC OCEAN

ANTARCTIC OCEAN

Tropic of Capricorn

Equator or Equinoctial Line

The Mail Route is Coloured thus

PLATE 39

John Tallis: The Eastern Hemisphere

Like Moule, John Tallis' Illustrated Atlas *reflects a movement away from the sombre scientific style that so typified early nineteenth-century mapmaking. Published to commemorate the Great Exhibition of 1851, Tallis' beautiful maps, engraved on steel by John Rapkin, reflect the glories of Britain's world empire and provide a pastiche of images of far-flung corners of the world available for the first time to the Victorian armchair traveller. (Private Collection)*

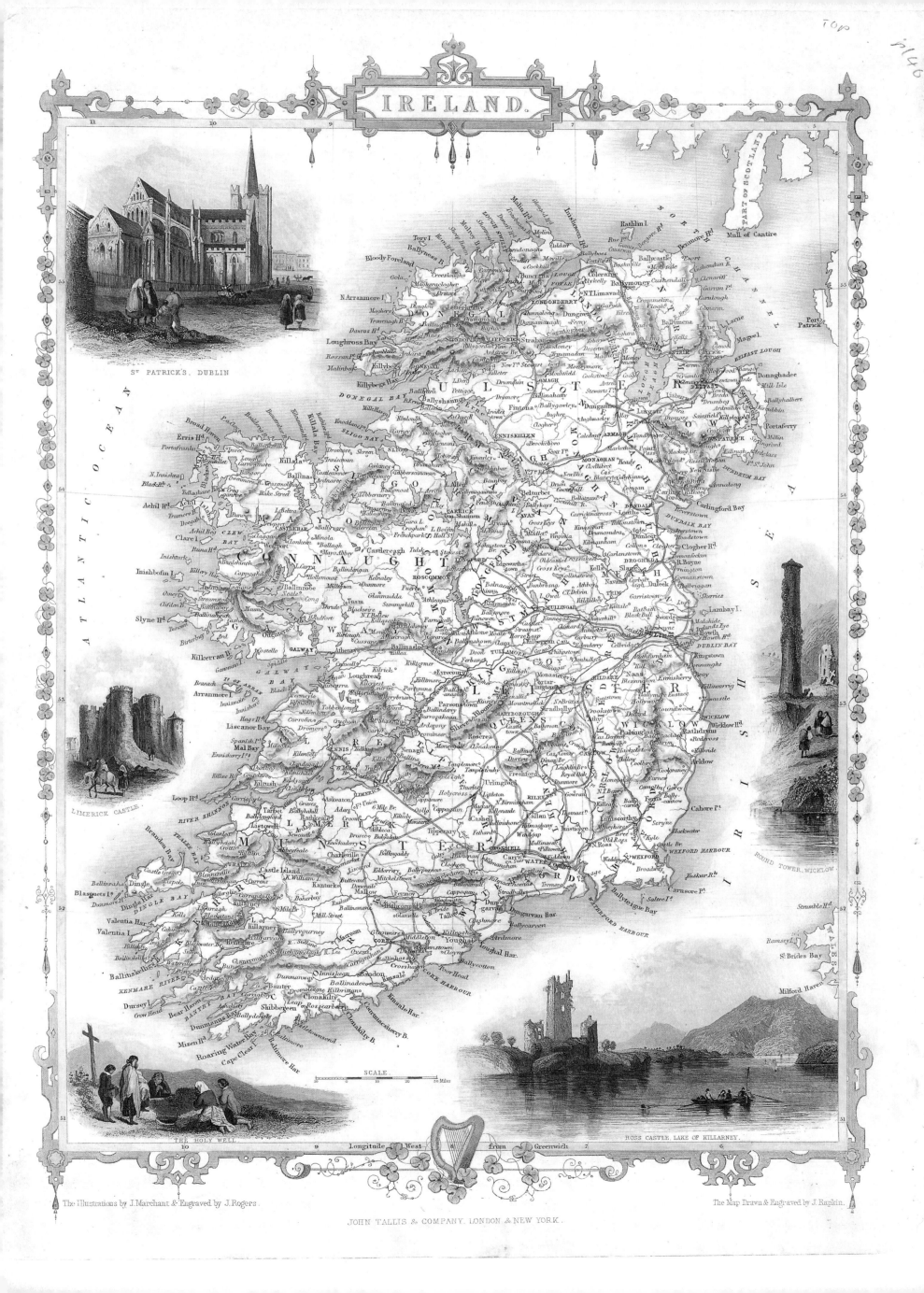

IRELAND.

ST PATRICK'S, DUBLIN.

LIMERICK CASTLE.

ROUND TOWER, WICKLOW.

THE HOLY WELL.

ROSS CASTLE, LAKE OF KILLARNEY.

SCALE.

Longitude West from Greenwich

The Illustrations by J. Marchant & Engraved by J. Rogers.

The Map Drawn & Engraved by J. Rapkin.

JOHN TALLIS & COMPANY, LONDON & NEW YORK.

PLATE 40
John Tallis: Ireland

John Tallis' companion map of Ireland from his Illustrated Atlas *(London, 1851) reveals the beauty and wildness of a country only just recovering from the effects of famine and emigration in the 1840s. With their foliate borders and scenic vignettes Tallis' maps are the final flourish in the craftsmanship and artistry of decorative antique maps. (Private Collection)*